Mary —
You a.
item.

MW00964109

MEETING MYSELF

Snippets from a Binging and Bulging Mind

Sept/9/13

BRENDA J. WOOD

All medical information is drawn only from the author's personal experience.

Author and Speaker Brenda J. Wood would love to hear from you!
Email: brendawoodauthor@yahoo.ca
Online: http://heartfeltdevotionals.wordpress.com
Facebook: www.facebook.com/brendawoodspeaker

ISBN 978-1-77069-444-6

Word Alive Press
131 Cordite Road, Winnipeg, MB R3W 1S1
www.wordalivepress.ca

WORD ALIVE PRESS
Just Write!

Printed in Canada

Library and Archives Canada Cataloguing in Publication

Wood, Brenda, 1945-
      Meeting myself : snippets from a binging and bulging mind / Brenda J. Wood.
ISBN 978-1-77069-444-6
      1. Wood, Brenda, 1945-. 2. Christian biography--Canada. 3. Bulimia--Patients--Biography. 4. Adult child abuse victims--Canada--Biography. 5. Authors, Canadian--Biography. I. Title.
BR1725.W66A3 2011   248.4   C2011-907839-2

For Ron, who walked with me every step of the way.

CHAPTER ONE

"Half of life is simply accepting what is."

I DIDN'T KNOW I WASN'T ME. How could I? As long as I could remember, I'd never been anyone else. That's what abuse did to me. Parts of me lay buried so deep that at first glance they seemed not to be there at all.

> Feelings? I don't have any. My life happens in the third person while I watch from afar. Experience teaches me that my feelings aren't safe. They repeatedly get me into trouble. Self-preservation stands between me and them. For safety's sake, they are sectioned off and twisted into plaits tighter than a seven-year-old child's pigtails. I want it to stay that way.

I met these startling words from my journal with shocked surprise. Where did they come from? Apparently, somewhere deep in my being lived a part of me I'd never confronted, let alone embraced. Long-buried memories lived a life sentence there with no parole. I'd seldom visited, but when this journal entry surfaced, it demanded dominance in my mind.

I didn't want to look that locked place in the face. It was too big to handle. It tripped me up, threw me down, and made me powerless. It turned my short-fused temper into a chocolate frenzy, a gluttonous binge or a bulimic episode.

I know friends and family didn't understand me or my attitudes, or even my actions. Why, I didn't even understand them myself. I'd come home from a function wondering why I'd said or done a certain thing. I couldn't put my finger on it, but I knew I flew on a different wavelength than the rest of the world. How is it that so many people lived inside my brain? Why did I see funny things as tragic and tragic things as laughable? Why on earth would I eat a full course meal, plus dessert, and then come home and eat a loaf of bread? Why was full never enough for me?

My problems looked a little different each time, but to me they could all be solved if I lost some weight. I consistently blamed everything on my eating habits, and the inevitable outcome. Fat. Forget the niceties of calling it overweight. Fat is where it's at for me.

Have a bout of cancer, or even two? No doubt they stemmed from my bad eating habits.

The first one took me by surprise. An innocent mole on my hand turned out to be stage-two melanoma. Two surgeries later, I found myself joining the sunless generation. No more sitting out with the family on pleasant days. No more picnics in the park. No more traipsing to Florida for a few weeks. No, now I clung to the inside of the house between 10:00 a.m. and 4:00 p.m. and wore sunscreen, sun-repellent hats, and suffocatingly hot clothing the rest of the time. Fun.

The next year, I developed a tumour in my parotid gland. The parotid glands are the largest of all the salivary glands. They secrete saliva into the mouth. Saliva helps us chew, swallow, and digest starches. Apparently, mumps actually happen in the parotids.

This second cancer surprised me, but it terrified me, too. Who am I kidding? It terrified me a lot. The diagnosis included warnings that I'd be disfigured, lose my ability to speak clearly, and perhaps even be paralyzed on my left side. The word "cancer" is scary enough, but I was a motivational speaker with her own company and TV show. What on earth would I do?

As it turned out, after surgery I had only two residuals. The first is a great profile which lets me look ten years younger on my left. This is the side I like to present to the camera!

The second is Frey's' Syndrome. I spell it "Fry's Syndrome." Only a foodaholic like me deserved something with a fat name. My symptoms include redness and sweating near the ear. Here's how it works. When I eat something really tasty—or even dream, think, or talk about it—my face leaks. I try to be discreet. I really do. However, if you see me swabbing at my dripping face, you can tell the meal was really great. The family loves to tease me with comments like, "So, I guess today's meal was superb. Mom is leaking." Or worse, "Gee Mom, if I'd known you hated my cooking that much I'd have ordered pizza."

The correct name for all that wetness is "gustatory sweating." As it was explained to me, the parotid nerves have to go somewhere, so they heal to the outside of the face. Just when you thought that was too much information, here's another tidbit for you: sometimes just smelling a particular food makes your nose run!

Can you follow my thinking? Fat person gets cancer on the hand that feeds her. Fat person gets cancer in the mouth area. Fat person gets Frey's Syndrome, a fat name if ever there was one. Fat person now displays her obsession with food by leaking water in every direction. Oh, if the fat person wasn't fat, fat person wouldn't get "fat" disease.

I knew where lots of our cash went. I spent a ton of money on my secret eating binges. One time, my husband Ron went away on a weeklong business trip. I dropped him at the airport and headed for a takeout place. Because I had two toddlers in the car, I justified buying three adult meals. Yes, of course, I ate every bite. Else why would I buy them? And I told myself that thin people never did that kind of thing and since I was fat… well, I had to.

House disorganized? Obviously, I ate too much and too often and didn't vacuum enough. Parents need full-time care? If I were thinner, I could lift them easier and we wouldn't need nurses. If I were at a healthy weight, I could keep them at home, take care of my own family, and even keep my full-time job. Instead I resigned them to a nursing home. Guilt. Everywhere, guilt.

If only I slimmed down to size ten. If only I didn't eat so much. If only I could lose weight. If only guilt didn't hook me into a deeper eating disorder.

Fat. Fat. Fat. That's me. I knew I was a compulsive eater, but I didn't know it had a name. Ed (eating disorder) and I dated on a regular basis. I saw food as the problem, but Ed married me and moved in long before I cared to admit his presence.

My parents hardly ever showed their feelings. Consequently, they didn't care to allow for ours. When my dog was killed on the road, I heard, "Stop crying over that stupid dog." That stupid dog annoyed Dad, but to me it seemed that Sport was the only one who ever listened to me.

When bullying continued at school, it was "Get over it. That's life. Stand up and tell them off." I was in Grade One. The bullies were in Grade Eight. Not likely.

This foodie discovered the soothing calm of food when my younger brother and sister disappeared for a morning. I ate, and then I ate some more. The relaxation that followed taught me that food could soothe any anxiety. It instantly became my coping mechanism and my available drug of choice.

Stress relief lay just out of reach in the kitchen cupboards, but it was captive to the rigid control of my mother's hands. I soon found ways around that. I needed a coping mechanism for the trauma of abuse, exams, conflict, dating issues, and all other childhood angst. I had no money, so those cupboard contents became my lifesavers. This wasn't as easy as it looked. Mom even kept count of the cheese slices. I began to sneak food under my mom's very nose. This involved considerable lying and manipulation, and I adapted quickly to my new lifestyle.

Don't have a date? Then eat your way to relaxation and peace. Studying hard for a history test? Pour your soul into a bag of chips. Every event or non-event needed a food source, and I continued to believe that if only I were thin… I'd…

By the time I figured out that Ed owned my hands, he'd already determined to possess my heart, mind, body, and soul. He gradually reeled me into the deep, and then deeper and deeper still. He was a deep sea fisherman and I swallowed his bait.

I silenced Ed's public image by eating tiny portions in company and only stealing food for my secret binges. I tormented myself with thoughts of self-hate, especially after a binging and purging episode. I avoided social contact as much as possible.

Because my weight numbers stood foremost in my mind, I always believed I would be a better person if only I were thin. I glared at life from an emotional standpoint, not a logical one. Sadly, I wasn't able to recognise that I was the only one preventing me from enjoying my life. Why couldn't I see that?

I teased myself into half-believing statements like, "Food eaten while standing up has no calories because it runs right out your toes onto the rug." That's why rugs need cleaning at least once a year. (This excuse worked better when shag carpet was in vogue.) Or how about these: "It takes a lot of energy to chew celery, but when you do, it cancels out dinner's calories. Foods eaten on holidays are calorie-free. Your friend will love you more if you eat her meal down to the last forkful. Have diet pop with your triple burger so that the drink can displace the fat. Ice cream is non-caloric if served with chocolate sauce. Food on the verge of spoiling is obviously fair game. Burnt food is a given and eating off other people's plates doesn't count if you only eat a forkful. Food eaten while lonely, sad, or afraid is washed away by your tears. Items imbibed in a holy setting are calorie-free if you are a member of the Church. Charity eating is for the good of the organization and therefore akin to the holiness rule (see above)."

Of course, I also believed that left-handed eaters lack dexterity, and since some of the food misses the mouth, it's a freebie. (Feel free to reverse this law if you are a right-handed eater).

On and on they went. "Stuff swallowed while you're in physical pain is a necessary comfort and may lower your blood pressure, something your doctor would surely recommend. You never keep track of stuff eaten beforehand, 'just in case' they have nothing at the party, or in case you get hunger pains or even homesick. Uneven edges must be cut, smoothed, and straightened. Serving jagged pie or sloppy cheese bits destroys your reputation as a homemaker. Mock Potato Salad, Pretend Pumpkin Pie, and No Noodle Lasagne are of no account because they aren't real."

Why would you even consider counting a teaspoon of crumbs or a finger full of peanut butter? Why leave leftover children's food on a plate when someone is starving in Asia? I don't think so.

And here's a big one: "Diets must begin on Monday." Starting every Monday, I sincerely promised to stop swallowing my own saliva and drip-dry the coffee.

Starting on Monday

Starting on Monday, I'll eat oil-less tuna.
Starting on Monday? No more French fries.
Starting on Monday, I'll be righteously honest.
Starting on Monday... it's no more food lies.

Once I even convinced myself that January 1 was the only decent day to start a weight-loss plan. I primed myself up for the year, ready to tackle my pounds with wild abandon. Unfortunately, the hostess at the New Year's Eve party didn't serve her culinary delights till 12:15 a.m. I ate. Surely you understand that it was just too late to lose weight at all that year...

Diet Spree by Me

It will not be too hard at all.
This diet's going to be a ball.
I clear the morning table of goodies once galore.
I swallow all the leftovers
And hunt around for more.
A gaping hole lies barren in the peanut butter jar.
I search about for chocolate. It surely can't be far.
High in cupboard where no one sees,
I find my stash of jujubes.
All is fair game in love and diet,
Till Monday when the scales riot.

It stands to reason that I got fatter. Subconsciously, say the experts, being overweight serves two purposes. It keeps men away and gives an illusion of strength and power. That may be true for some, but I can't say that I thought it to be true for myself. Over the years, my body rebelled by taking on everything from sciatica to gall bladder, hiatal hernia, and heart scares. Oh yes, you guessed it. If only I wasn't fat, I wouldn't have this problem. (And by the way, you can die from basic Ed.)

The journal knows.

Grief and anger rush over me as I think about the little girl I'd been before my abuser took myself away from me. Did I say *my* abuser? No. I will not let him own me in any way. Let him own himself, his evil, his sin. Let his tentacles untwine from my soul. Physically, he's done just that. He is dead, but not to me. Emotionally, he lingers on, stacking fear into every fraction of my life. Even in his absence he leaves fear—absurd, irrational fear.

Fear dictates my life. I cope by eating until fear, loneliness, sadness, happiness, (name feeling at will) calms me. I stuff down every emotion before it escapes. If I trust my emotions, I'll experience the abuse all over again. I fear the outcome of that. I don't have the strength for it. In spite of my determination not to feel anything, I am a place of living terror.

Occasionally, the evening news relays the story of a deer jumping through a plate glass window or a bear forcing its way into a neighbourhood cottage. I always thought those made for a charming news story, until it happened to me.

Our farmhouse stood in a bush-like setting of almost fifty trees. (We'd planted them after my granny bemoaned their absence.) Anyway, after a few years of growth, such a grove attracted abundant wildlife. I loved them all, especially because they were outside and I was not. The location cried out peace, safety, and protection. At least, it did until "the thing" broke in.

I made the children put on every piece of protective gear we owned. Picture three cowering people huddled in everything from hockey helmets to high-top rubber boots, and armed with baseball bats, hockey sticks, and brooms. As if that weren't enough, I insisted we perch on the second-storey stairs, because on the television news, wild critters don't climb stairs.

I left the outside door open. Perhaps that four-legged horror would leave on its own. Did I mention it was winter? We spent a long, cold, hungry, and scary −22°C day arrayed on those steps. Our conversation was sparse and our tummies rumbled with hunger, but I remained ever vigilant, ready to flee at any moment should the animal make for us. I couldn't call for help, because the phone was out of reach.

The bathroom, too, remained at a distance. When nature called, I marshalled the children into a small but obedient army. Then we marched our way to the facilities and back, all the while screaming and stamping our feet so as to keep the monster at bay.

I was terrified. I was responsible for my kids' lives. How could I explain their injury, or even death, to their dad? My kids were only annoyed. They were young enough to think they could face any danger and live. To humour me, though (and because they were more afraid of me than they were of the critter), they stayed on those stairs.

Hours later, my unsuspecting husband came home from work to find his wife screaming from the stairway though the open door.

"Help! Watch out! Be careful! Get the weapons! This critter has been in here all day!"

Hubby went for the big guns. He grabbed the appropriate weapons while our teenagers welcomed their dad with open arms. They sighed in relief at being freed from the bondage of the stairs. Then they helped their dad set the mouse trap.

See what I mean? A mouse kept me prisoner in my own home. A mouse! As a child, I entertained a family of pet mice. I found them in the wheat field after Dad combined the crop and I kept them in a child-size wheelbarrow on a bed of straw. I played with them long after they died. Give me a break, I was only six. Anyway, a century later, after being abused, the adult Brenda panicked at the mere glimpse of a mouse.

That's the kind of craziness my husband and children lived with on a daily basis. Any change of routine increased the strain on my already chaotic mind.

I recouped from that terrible day by swallowing half a roast, a quart or two of congealed gravy, and some cold boiled turnip. I didn't particularly like turnip when it was hot, but binge eating does not demand quality ingredients.

> An idea in my head becomes a deed done. That's how I live. That's how I eat. Some past thought crosses my mind and, without examining it for common sense, I binge. Taste is never an issue. Cold mashed potatoes, ice cream, and dry bread are all the same to me. I never choose raw or crunchy foods, because they refuse to be rushed. They take too long to eat. They don't drown emotional pain fast enough. They are a waste.

I prefer hot food.

Reigned On

Soft drizzles mist through the air,
Dancing life into delicate petals below.
Do those petaled beauties accept this generous gift?
Extending their stamens to catch and swallow?

Or do tiger lilies flounce their jaws fiercely,
Fighting off life-giving sustenance?
And lilies choke as their cup-like shapes
Gag on more than their share?

Will marigolds bristle with complaint
At the inconvenience and bother,
While pansies stir their faces
Into frowning, fighting attitudes?

Have they threatened the heavens
With fist-like leaves and an angry cry?
No! They understand, far better than I,
That though life rains, it need not reign.

Will I ever learn that, like my flowers,
I can soak in all that life brings
And see it for the growing necessity that it is,
Rather than letting rain reign over me?

CHAPTER TWO

"I was twenty-five before I found out that

gravy was not a beverage."

THERE ARE TWO KINDS OF people in the world: gluttons and non-gluttons. Since I am a slightly recovered glutton, I feel qualified to point out the vast differences between the two. Non-gluttons don't hide chocolate in their toilet tanks, between the mattress and the box spring, in laundry hampers, or in the glove box of the car. They throw out stale potato chips, eat only one peanut at a time, and never celebrate holidays by eating ice cream under the dash of their car. They may straighten a curtain, but never a block of cheddar or slice of pie. Not for them cold gravy sandwiches, aged green potato salads, or entire chocolate cakes at one sitting. They don't make chocolate chip cookies just so they can eat the dough.

Grandpa brought us chocolate Easter bunnies. I gobbled mine and started in on Larry's. This two-year-old foolishly trusted his four-year-old sister. I squished the bunny's ears.

"You don't want to eat broken bunny ears, do you, Larry?"

"Nooo," he gasped.

I ate them. Poke!

"You don't want to eat broken bunny tummy, do you, Larry?"

"Noooo," he cried in horror.

I gobbled my bunny and most of his. Mom caught me before I got the tail.

The journal continues:

> Was I born with food issues? One might think so from stories like this. Was I abused at such an early age that I can't remember? How else can I explain such a voracious appetite? I am always hungry. Enough food for the average person is never enough for me.
>
> Mom does the food shopping and prepares all the meals. She knows every morsel in the cupboard, fridge, and cold storage. She knows who to ask when a cheese slice goes missing or a cupcake disappears. Why is it always me? Why do I have this voracious appetite and the five other people in our family do not? Or do they and they hide it better than I do?

"Take a tart for yourself and one for Larry," said Mom. I took the tarts alright, right out to the alcove at the front step. I gobbled them both down, not even tasting their juicy sweetness. I needed their comfort, not their flavour. Secure in the knowledge that I'd succeeded, I strolled my eight-year-old self back into the kitchen, only to find that rascal Larry asking if he could have a tart. My irate mother rightly accused me of stealing. All that great food and my taste buds remembered not a smidge or swallow of it.

I relished my responsibility as official lunch-maker. Ever searching for ways to get more to eat, I sliced all their sandwiches in half and took a sliver off each cut side. This worked well until less starving family members brought home uneaten food. This puzzled me. How could anyone not eat whatever food was in hand?

Anyway, one day Mom called me on it. "Those sandwiches are awfully narrow," she commented gently. Not to be outwitted, I simply started cutting the bread a little off side and sneaking one slice out of the middle instead of two.

Marriage and my own kitchen created more eating opportunities. Now I was in charge of the cheese slices, the roast, the pie, and whatever else my little heart desired. A pie served one evening became part of my next day's binge. Cook enough for two meals? Sure… and eat the second one for a snack.

Greed was never my intention. I always started with love of family in mind. I wanted to give them the best. I always sampled, to be sure. What did it matter if I'd made the recipe a dozen times? Today might be the first failure.

The stove, the refrigerator, and I were intimate buddies. I found that I could swallow quite a bit of yummy with them near my tummy. One bonus day, I made chocolate fudge that just would not set. I ladled it into a pan and then into the fridge. I saved time by putting a tablespoon in there as well. Open the door to get milk? I scooped fudge into my face. It turned out to be an easily solved mathematical problem. Every door opening equalled one spoonful of fudge. Voila!

I only ever intended a teensy little taste of the freshly-baked chocolate cake. It was another of those tried and true recipes. I started with the sliver of all slivers… almost infinitesimal, you might say. Well, at least I would say that, but honestly, you can't tell what chocolate tastes like from a teensy little taste.

The sliver became a slice, and the slice became a wedge, and the wedge became a quarter of the cake. By the time my feverishly fearful feelings settled, half the cake had disappeared. Honestly, I looked at that plate with shock. Even though I knew I'd eaten it, in some strange way that cake had eaten me.

Now, I don't know about you, but I couldn't tell my family that I'd eaten half a cake. Right off, they'd be wondering how I could eat so much, and secondly, they'd be wondering how I could even tell them that.

I come from a frugal background. I'd been taught that someone in Africa or India, or some other place, was starving for food. No, I couldn't throw it out. Surely that was a sin. No point in getting God mad at me, too, right?

I couldn't throw it out, because I was raised on waste-not-want-not. I did what I could to help a bad situation. I polished it off. As God is my witness, I didn't even burp. Often, I'd bake two desserts, eat one and serve one at the family dinner table. A whole apple pie, a two-layer chocolate cake with date filling… it didn't matter that I didn't like pie or date filling. I just needed swallowable servings of anything. More than once, I'd eat a full dinner of whatever was on the menu long before we sat to table. Then I managed to stuff down another couple of helpings. The memory gags me now.

I baked chocolate chip cookies just so I could eat the dough. No one seemed to notice that a six-dozen cookie recipe shrunk to only two dozen in our house. I gobbled the middles out of nine-by-thirteen pans of Chelsea buns and brownie bars, shoved the rest into eight-inch square pans, and cried, "Look what I made for you!"

Always in martyr mode, I insisted on clearing the dinner table alone. This gave me freedom to sop up scads of gravy with leftover bread or even drink the gravy boat dry. I was twenty-five before I found out that gravy was not a beverage.

Hiding food in toilet tanks made perfect sense to me. I'd store chocolate goodies in leak-proof bags, attach them to the cross bar, and haul them out at will. Intimate private moments always included some kind of gobbling.

Don't judge me too harshly. After all, this was a "green" thing to do. We used less water every time we flushed. I found this habit especially rewarding because teenagers don't look for food in bathrooms or, for that matter, behind tinned asparagus in the pantry.

I learned great food lessons from well-meaning fat friends. Not only did we share food sale information, but we also shared new ways to get more food to eat. For example, family won't look for special treats in freezer containers carefully marked "liver."

One gal used to hide chocolate bars between her mattress and box spring. After a 3:00 a.m. bathroom break, she'd nibble away.

Years passed. Hubby never noticed. One night, though, he heard paper rustling and wanted to know what was going on. Of course, he demanded a share of the chocolate bar.

My friend puzzled on this all day. How could she keep up her early morning binges but still keep all the food for herself? Her "aha" moment resulted in slyly hiding her candy bars, as usual, between the box spring and the mattress… but first she removed the paper. After all, lint has no calories.

I did all these things and others too painful and, yes, even too shameful to share.

Soon I birthed a new fear. What would I do if I got bigger than I already was? There were scary signs that my weight was out of control. One day, I heard the slap-slap-slapping sound of footsteps behind me as I climbed the stairs. I thought someone had broken into the house. I stopped. The noise stopped. I walked. The noise began. Finally, I figured it out; it was just the sound of my thighs flapping together.

I began to write "fat" poetry like this:

The Dieter's Lament

The sleeves are bulging in my dress.
My bra is double-rolled.
The calories I ate at lunch
Have multiplied untold.
My pantyhose are at half-mast
And cutting off my veins.
My extra fifty pounds or so
Are giving knee joint pains.

My waistline is herniated
By the elastic in my dress
And as I speak, a button pops,
My own fault I do confess.
My underwear is crying out
From definite overstrain.
My arches falling to my sole
Surely need a crane.

When waving bye to all my friends,
My arm did slap my face.
I've switched to slip-on shoes this week.
I can't reach to tie a lace…

Obviously, I couldn't see my world clearly. Yes, I was overweight, but exaggerations like these did little for my self-esteem or my reality.

Food kept my painful feelings and memories in check. The world saw a perfect, polite, obedient Brenda. The real me was a fearful manipulator, completely devoid of self-esteem. Some of my mom's scrupulously honest conscience had rubbed off on me. Well, in almost all areas of my life but food. When it came to food, you couldn't believe a word I said.

I craved peace at any price and paid any price to get it. I learned to avoid conflict if at all possible. I swallowed unkind, rude comments and heaped them into my already overloaded mind for future review. I felt insecure, afraid, unlovable, and depressed. I couldn't cope with my multiplying fears, so I used food and weight to numb them. I spent all my energy and resources trying to make my outside look good. *my home, my kids*

I think our hearts can get fat just like any other area of our bodies. They expand beyond normal size, just like our hips. Let's call it what it is: they get unhealthily *fat!* A heart bloats and becomes fat when it's heavy with grief, stress, hurt, and loss. We jump at the first cure that comes to mind—sweets, drugs, cigarettes, whatever—only to discover that they result in more heart heaviness. The truth is that only God can size up a heart and lead it in the way it should go. I was a long way from figuring this out.

I try diet after diet. Some are worse than others. The grapefruit diet, the cabbage soup diet, no protein, all protein, low-carbohydrate, high carbohydrate, sanctimonious fasting, and the latest celebrity diet... they all pass through my brain, and sometimes through my lips. The results are always the same. Denial brings on binges with a vengeance and leaves utter disdain for both diet and required food. None have any lasting effect.

I decided to write my own weight loss plan. After all, who knew me better than me? Astoundingly, this led to my own quite successful weight loss business. That old saying— "those who can, do, and those who can't, teach"—appeared to be absolutely true in my case.

I still didn't understand that food soothed the savage angry beast within me and that my weight was my armour of self-protection. I didn't understand that true change happens from the inside out.

No one told me there was a God who loved me enough to take away my fear. I didn't know He had said, *"Fear not [there is nothing to fear], for I am with you; do not look around you in terror and be dismayed, for I am your God. I will strengthen and harden you to difficulties, yes, I will help you; yes, I will hold you up and retain you with My [victorious] right hand of righteousness and justice"* (Isaiah 41:10).

I didn't know God cared more about the inner me than He did the outer me. *"For the Lord sees not as man sees; for man looks on the outward appearance, but the Lord looks on the heart"* (1 Samuel 16:7).

Instead, I continually judged myself by worldly standards. Since I couldn't control my eating; I decided to get rid of any food I swallowed. Years passed before I learned that "it" was an addictive, life-threatening disease called bulimia. I found out only by accident when I happened upon an article about a jockey who did what I did. If this weird act had a name and others did it, too, then it must be normal... right?

"Thank God I'm not alone," I whispered. "I'm not so bad after all... am I?"

> Hoss, my dachshund, has an identity crisis. I think it's because he's been parented by our two Scotch collies. He goes everywhere they go. He mimics their behaviour. Somewhere in his doggy brain, he sees himself as a collie. I've tried placing him directly in front of the mirror, but Hoss does not want to acknowledge his real image.[1]

Hoss and I had a lot in common. I needed to look in the mirror and see myself the way God saw me. That's easier said than done.

I didn't yet understand that I would never be able to live my life as a success if I still saw myself as a failure. The two sides of me needed to mesh. Better still, one of us had to go.

1 Phipps, Lynne. "The Mirror." *Daily Devotional.* Date of Access: November 28, 2011 (http://daily.presbycan.ca/devotions/2010/10-07-13.html).

CHAPTER THREE

"The difficult thing about memories is

remembering them."

THOUSANDS OF DOLLARS went in and out of my mouth over the years, money stolen from my family in the way of binged food and bulimic habits. Gallons of ice cream, truckloads of bread, and chocolate by the grocery cart made their way in and out of my body. They lived a vivid, but short recycled life.

Again, the journal is my witness.

> Shall I tell of long, tortuous binges that filled my day, interspersed with small bouts of normal living? I'm feeling especially awful today and prepared for a binge of grilled cheese. I made up nearly a loaf of bread and opened my mouth for that first relieving bite. Unexpected company signaled their presence with a knock at the door. I dove for cover with plate in hand. The cupboard under the kitchen sink was the only place large enough to hide the evidence.

After dinner, that spectacle rose to greet us all when I reached for the dish soap.

It doesn't take much to set me off. A misconstrued line or two of conversation and I'm a goner. Last week, a relative made a statement that most days I would find quite inoffensive. It was really a nothing comment, but I took it personally. (That's what happens when the memories get too close to the surface.)

Of course, I didn't reply. Instead, the Queen of Sandwiches waited for an opportune moment, rushed to the kitchen, and assembled and gobbled down a frozen bologna sandwich. I made it back to the family room before the television commercial was over, mustard stains and telltale crumbs barely visible.

A sandwich queen has researched and understands all that is necessary to gorge on bread and butter. Bread must be quick to chew. No whole wheat or twelve-grain stuff for the bulimic. Butter should preferably be soft, but if not, wide slices of it cover a slice of bread just as well. (The advent of soft margarine made my day!)

I tell the family that we freeze luncheon meats individually for easier lunch-making and they believe me. Actually, I do it so that in my desperation I can grab a slice and inhale it.

I'm also an expert on freezing. Most sweets never completely freeze through. Butter tarts make my teeth a little itchy on the way down, but their middles aren't too hard to chew. Did I say chew? Chew? Who has time to chew? The goal is to force stuff down before my emotions force their way up.

I eat raw batter by the ladle. Cake mixes seldom get to be a double layer in my home. They are only

small, eight-inch pans. The rest of the batter is in
me. The threat of raw eggs or uncooked flour never
crosses my mind. No wonder I had gallstone surgery
at age twenty-two.

The local variety store sells chocolate bars by the dozen.
I buy a pack, then eat nine while taking the long way home.
Sometimes I have to park on the side of the road in order to
eat them all before I get to the house. I hide the wrappers in
my purse and present the three remaining bars to the family. They are always coconut, the kind I only eat when really
desperate.

You might think I have no self-control. On the contrary,
I have plenty, even if it's only in certain areas. Self-control
kept me alive and prevented me from being worse than I
was. It kept me from killing myself because I couldn't stand
the suffering. I thought about taking up booze as a comforter. When I told Ron, he begged me, "Honey, please don't do
it." Common sense, always one of my strong points, took
hold. I already had a problem with food. No point in expanding my issues!

One day, planning a walk down the back lane of the
farm with Baby in carriage, I cradled a butcher knife in my
hands while seriously thinking of suicide. I almost tucked
it under the carriage mattress. At the last minute, I decided
not to take it with us, but only because I was afraid no one
would know where to look for the baby. Suicide, you ask?
Yes, anything to stop the emotional pain.

By this time, I'd told Ron the bare bones of my story.
However, he had no idea what lurked just beneath the crevice of my outside calm. My close friends, Binging and Purging, continued their job as my salvation.

No one can ever accuse me of sweetening the story. My journals tell the whole truth and nothing but the truth. The pages speak.

> I am "worshipping" on my knees with head in toilet after another binge. I wish it were only for the cleaning of such, but no, it's my compelling desire to throw up everything I've eaten. It's been a particularly bad week. Yesterday, I felt so lost and alone. I ate everything in sight, set no priorities for the day, and accomplished nothing. I am captive to this awful habit. I need help, but there's nowhere to turn. If I did, I'd have to admit what I do. Does it even have a name? This disgusting habit on its own is unbelievable. If I couple that with my cravings and my compulsion to perform it, people will think I'm nuts. Sometimes I think I'm crazy. I'm ashamed. There is no way out.
>
> This is a new toilet in a different colour, but it performs the same duty. The other lavender one shattered when I knocked a jar of bath salts off the shelf during an unpremeditated "episode." When Ron asked how it happened, I told him the truth. He made a face, bought a new one, installed it, and never mentioned it again.

Since lavender no longer held sway in the decorating world, we had to get a white toilet. Every time I enter that room, the glaring evidence of my mental failure stares me in the face.

As a child, I used to dream of my perfect Prince Charming. I expected he would be tall, dark, and handsome. His great paying job would be clean and effortless. Not for him the risk of farming, like the other men in our little community. Not for him the long slavish hours of working off the farm to make ends meet. No, he would have a lovely, safe, white-collar job. He would only work from nine to five, and then he would come home and dedicate his every spare moment to me, my needs, and the needs of our six children. I'd never seen a white picket fence, but I wanted one, like the ones they had on all the television shows. I knew how life was supposed to be. I intended to be a lawyer and my Prince Charming would have to line his life up with mine.

Then I met Ron. Tall? Not so much. Dark and handsome? Well, in a rugged sort of Elvis Presley way. Great job? Starving farmer. Ate with his pinky finger in the air? No, he relished every mouthful. Liked opera? Ha! It was country music, all the way. Slaved on the farm to make ends meet? Yes.

It wasn't that I didn't have warning or time to look for someone else. I fell in love with him when I was still in grade school, long before he noticed me. (He denies this, but I know better!)

He'd stop at our local country school after giving his horse, Tillie, her daily run. He looked so dashing, so exciting, and a little bit dangerous, too, setting astride that big brown mare. He didn't see me, though. While all the other students clustered around him, I only peeked out the classroom door.

Our actual courtship began at the Strawberry Festival, the summer of my sixteenth birthday. I only went to eat, but as small town affairs work, I eventually found myself in the back, helping with the dishes.

Ron came into the room, turned to hand me a tea towel, and time literally stood still. Even though I sensed people staring at us, I couldn't seem to move. Nor could he. For the longest moment, I gazed into those dancing blue eyes and he into mine. Finally, I shook myself from my trance and took that towel. He was twenty-six.

Needless to say, my parents weren't pleased. Ron was the local "bad boy." Now, in our day, that meant he went to all the dances, drank some, and even smoked a bit. Oh, we were the talk of the town. In fact, when we married two years later, some people wouldn't even contribute to the community collection for our wedding gift. My mom put voice to their words: "You've wasted your life, Brenda. You could have been somebody. Now you are going to live on that broken down farm, with that guy, and starve to death."

If I'd made a list of reasons to marry Ron and checked them against my original list, he would never have made it. Yes, he did all the things I didn't like.

"Never mind," I said to myself. "I can change all that."

Ron was everything else I wanted to be—good-humoured and fun to be with, tender-hearted, befriended and friendly, and not afraid to be in or speak to crowds. The real reason I married Ron? I sensed somehow that he would keep me safe.

We lived in edgy, near-starvation mode for a couple of years until Ron changed careers.

I thought, *This is for me.* He chose mechanics—not so clean, not so high-paying. I still hoped for other changes, so I nagged and dragged! That is, I talked too much and took him to places he didn't care about.

I exposed him to Shakespeare while he encouraged me to watch wrestling. He loved the outdoors, his snowmobile, construction, and tinkering with old engines while I yearned for a good book and a warm fire.

One day, as my friends and I whined about our husbands not making their own lunch (among other things), a recent widow whispered softly, "I'd give anything to make my husband's lunch today."

Oh.

And I realized that I'd really met my prince all those years ago. Looking a little different? Yes. Acting a little different? Yes. Loving me unconditionally? Yes. Loved unconditionally in return? Finally, yes.

Prince Ronald was my first safe place, the first person I told about the abuse and the one who comforted me after those terrifying nightmares.

Journaling on.

> The toilet event confirms my belief that I have nowhere to turn. The best part of marriage is being with someone who understands you. The worst part of marriage is being with someone who understands you. No one wants to address the issue, and that includes me. I'm safer in here, inside myself, locked in the disjointed room that pictures the double-minded me. The white toilet in a lavender bathroom stands as a silent witness to what I call <u>my dis-ease. It's not a disease like cancer, but like cancer it irritates, permeates, and regulates me in body and soul.</u>

The Bible says, *"Do not conform to the pattern of this world, but be transformed by the renewing of your mind. Then you will be able to test and approve what God's will is—his good, pleasing and perfect will"* (Romans 12:2, NIV).

What did that mean? Would God just cut my mind out and put something better in there? No such luck. I couldn't figure out how this worked, and no one else seemed to know, either.

> The unheated cold half of our drafty old farmhouse rivals the temperature of a deep freezer. We store overflow food on a side table in this chilly living

room. Right now, it holds holiday leftovers. The phrase "turkey sandwich" pops into my head. I brace for the temperature. Then I think, *God is supposed to be able to help people with things like this.*

I kneel down the way people do in Sunday school pictures and pray, "God, keep me from eating this food." All the while, I'm thinking about white meat on buttered white bread, cranberry sauce, double mayo, and stuffing.

I gave God about ten seconds to act. Would the turkey disappear? Maybe I'd develop a sudden loathing for white meat. The phone might ring! Perhaps a neighbour would come over? Nothing happened.

"Well," I sighed aloud, "I didn't think that would work."

The rest is history. I didn't know that I didn't have to think on every thought that dropped into my mind, or even that I could choose my thoughts. The thought of walking away never crossed my mind. Like Hoss, I didn't recognise who I was. The Bible said that I was God's child, but I was a really slow believer.

The journal tells what I did think about.

Do abusers ever care about their victims? Do they just want what they want when they want it, and it happened to be you or me because we happened to be there? Do they ever fathom the depths of the soul they permeate? Do they know they destroy lives? Do they care? I doubt it.

Do they have any conscience? Are they haunted by their actions on the innocent? Do they rationalize that they are the abused and put upon? Wouldn't they have to? How else can they live in their skin? I hear that the abuser has been abused and that's why they do what they do. Someone who experienced this pain wants to inflict it on another? You have got to be kidding! Do abusers care that they leave a shattered person behind? I doubt it. If they did, surely they would never abuse. Would they?

CHAPTER FOUR

"Living under the circumstances

put me over the edge."

SOME REMINISCE ABOUT their poor family background and say things like, "We were really poor, but we didn't know it." I want to know how that happened.

The usual family worries were present in my parents' home. "Get more money. We don't have enough money. How will we pay these bills? No, we can't afford that." And I took it all to mean, "Don't ask us for anything. We don't have it."

I was in charge one day when my sister cut her foot badly. The neighbour helping us insisted that twelve-year-old me make the decision on whether or not she should go to the doctor. "You're the adult," I wanted to shout. "How can you expect a twelve-year-old to know what to do? Why don't you tell me? Totally unfair! I'm only twelve!" But I said nothing. My ears rang with the "we have no money" litany and I dreaded what Mom would say if I spent any.

When they came home hours later, I got a lecture all right. Only it went like this: "Why didn't you take care of your sister? Why didn't you get her to the doctor?"

Again, I said nothing. Children weren't allowed to talk back, let alone shout, in our family. But I wanted to shout out, "You tell me all the time that we have no money! I'm only twelve! Why should I have to make this decision? Where were the adults?"

I knew that answer. They weren't there for me during the abuse and they weren't going to be there now. Adults did not protect little children. It was too hard for them. At that moment, I gave up any thought of telling my parents about the abuse. I knew they'd see me as the one at fault. I made a conscious decision to keep all my thoughts and feelings to myself forever. I decided to be in charge of my own life, as much as possible, from that moment on.

I didn't mind wearing second-hand clothes; we got lots of them. But people had to know that most wouldn't fit me. Why did they give me their daughter's skinny stuff when I wasn't skinny? Comments from others didn't help. "Wearing other people's old clothes? You aren't that poor, are you?" I guess we were.

One uncle cruelly offered his opinion of my thirteen-year-old looks, size, and future at the crowded family dinner table.

"That one," he commented as he nodded at my younger, thinner, prettier eight-year-old sister, "has it all over that one." And he pointed his finger at me.

Of course, I realize now that was a thoughtless, stupid, unkind, and even untrue remark, but, as an abused child, I believed him that day—and for many years to follow. Maybe he was speaking my personal thoughts aloud. Since no one, not even my parents, rebuked him, I added it to the angst of my already beleaguered soul. I chalked it up as one more reason to keep to myself.

I seldom asked for money and I learned not to ask for time. My parents had none to spare. The abuser was a family acquaintance, as so many are. My parents spent more time with him than with me. I took that to mean that they cared more about him than they did about me.

> I am always restless, never at peace. Eating tamps down pain, but it never stays there. It surfaces as projectile vomit. I am beginning to understand it's a feverish need to rid myself of rage, filth, and memories. After these frenzied moments, I repeatedly consider my history. Oh, I am angry, but mostly at myself for not making someone listen. Some heard, but no one actually listened. Again, I ask, who would listen?
>
> When I finally told a doctor, he promptly declared that my abuse wasn't violent enough or prolonged enough to be a problem. He declared it to be a non-issue. I guess it was… for him.
>
> Ron knows. He says he loves me anyway, but I consider myself damaged goods. How can his heart not feel cheated? I don't care about myself. How can I believe that anyone else does?

I fear hunger. I know clock hunger, head hunger, and mouth hunger, but not stomach hunger. It seems to me that I've been sneaking, binging, and rebuking food for a lifetime.

The bulimia exploded forth for the first time in the midst of my safe and happy marriage. It simply topped up the more visible struggles of a nervous breakdown, irrational fear, guilt, chronic worry, depression, diet pills, and life-threatening illnesses. I was a person without hope.

I took small comfort from the fact that I never actually stole from outsiders to feed my habit. Not for me the raiding of grocery shelves, stuffing food into my mouth in broad daylight and leaving the used packages discarded on the shelves. It didn't occur to me that I was stealing money, time, and love from my family.

Someone once asked Italian music conductor Arturo Toscanini what ranked as his most important achievement. He said that there was no such thing. Author Andy Andrews calls this the Butterfly Effect, or the law of sensitive dependence upon initial conditions.[2]

The idea is that <u>everything you do matters</u>. That means my abuse and my eating disorders made a difference in the world. Why wouldn't they? They certainly made a difference to me. Even today, some of my handwriting traits point toward my past.

Since I still believed that fat was my problem, I set out to become a food and diet expert. The search for my hundred-pound fat suit began in earnest.

"How are you doing?" a man once asked his friend.

"Oh, I'm all right, under the circumstances," replied the friend.

"Well, what are you doing under there?"

It was many long years before I understood that <u>God is faithful in the good times and also in the bad times</u>. When <u>the way is rough, your faith has a chance to grow.</u>

---

2 Andrews, Andy. *The Butterfly Effect* (Nashville, TN: Thomas Nelson, 2009).

Under the Circumstances (by Edith V. Wood)

Under the circumstances,
We often hear folks say,
And truly there are many
As we go along life's way.

Sickness, pain and suffering,
Hurts of every kind,
Losses, problems, pressures,
Strain—body, soul and mind.

Under the circumstances,
Is a stressful place to be.
Faith is dampened, hopes are crushed,
The light we cannot see.

Above the circumstances
Is where God would have us dwell.
Where simple faith reminds us
That He doeth all things well.[3]

It's been said that when you reach the end of your rope, you should tie a knot and hang on. I got to the end of my rope. I suffered continuous depression. I had a nervous breakdown. I thought I'd lose my mind because of the pain, the habits, and the memories pouring over me. Thankfully, somebody gave me the knot for my rope. Somebody told me about Jesus. This Jesus knew all about my fears and failures, yet He loved me unconditionally. In fact, He loved me so much that He died on the cross just for me. He rose from the dead just for me! If I would ask Him to come into my life, He'd send His Holy Spirit to live in me. All I had to do was turn from my old life, ask Him to forgive me, and ask Him to come into my life. And I did that very thing.

3   Used by permission.

I cautiously began to accept these truths and started the journey of learning that my self-esteem doesn't originate in myself. It comes from who I am in the Lord Jesus Christ.

CHAPTER FIVE

"You have to find out for yourself that

Jesus is enough."

SINCE I ASKED JESUS INTO my life, I've had my share of mountaintop experiences and answered prayer. Who hasn't? The trouble is that mountains overshadow valleys. They don't always remove them. My mountain-climbing looked more like an eternal stay in base camp.

When I found out what God had to say about sin and gluttony, I added that guilt to a relationship that was supposed to free me from both. I stumbled over Bible verses like these:

> Anyone, then, who knows the good he ought to do and doesn't do it, sins. (James 4:17, NIV)

> But the man who has doubts is condemned if he eats, because his eating is not from faith; and everything that does not come from faith is sin. (Romans 14:23, NIV)

This last one kicked me in the teeth, and by the time I read Proverbs 23:2, I was a goner: *"And put a knife to your throat if you are given to gluttony"* (NIV).

Yikes. I journaled my frustration:

> It is clear to me that I am in deep sin do-do with God. I looked up the dictionary definition of sin. Sin: "any voluntary transgression of the law of God." Good grief.
>
> You'd think I'd have the sense to stop there. No. I searched out the definition of gluttony. Gluttony: "extravagant indulgence of the appetite for food."
>
> My hubby was right when he told me that if others couldn't make me feel bad, I'd do it by punishing myself. Why not go for broke and check out bulimia, too?
>
> Bulimia means to have hunger like an ox. It is a condition in which bouts of overeating are followed by undereating, the use of laxatives, or self-induced vomiting. It is insatiably eating thousands of calories at one sitting (and, I might add, a mighty short sitting), followed by purging the food from the body in some way. Symptoms include unexpressed anger, perfectionism, and a lack of self-esteem. I am guilty of all three. God is supposed to be a forgiving God. Does God forgive me for even this? I doubt it.

I was a Christian for four years before it came to me that perhaps bulimia wasn't a real God-pleaser. I'd been its captive for sixteen years. When Jesus gave me the strength and the courage to give it up, both the journal and I were surprised.

I'd been a regular guest on a local TV show, and when I planned the content for our next taping, I had no idea that show would be the beginning of my physical freedom.

Camera! Lights! Big mouth!

The interviewer and I blithely discussed eating disorders... and then I paused and added the comment that would change my life forever.

"I know of which I speak because I am bulimic."

I don't know who was more surprised, the extremely professional interviewer or her guest. Somehow I muddled through to the end and scrambled to the parking lot. Thousands watched as I bared my soul. Well, actually they wouldn't watch for a couple more hours because we always taped ahead. I had time. I dashed home in a panic.

> I'd never intended a public audience for my confessional. I'd never intended to confess ever, but after sixteen years of silent obedience to this thing, God gave me the courage to open it to the light. I shudder at the thought of Ron and the children seeing my confession. How would they take it? What would they think of me?
>
> I played the tape. No reaction at all. I queried them individually. Nothing. Finally, one admitted that they had known all along. And they blamed themselves because they thought they were the cause. My guilt multiplies.

In a physical sense, bulimia no longer owned me. My inside life still spiralled out of control, but business success softened the pain a little. I started my own weight-loss company, wrote and published several cookbooks, and became a popular motivational speaker. A television series followed. When my husband and children asked Jesus into their lives, I thought life was as good as it could get.

And then, at the very same time that I had my first cancer surgery, a work accident left Ron critically ill. Because his jaw was broken in ten places, that meant pureed food and family financial distress for six weeks.

> Oh well, pile it on, Brenda. Don't share with Hubby your fears and turmoil. No, he has enough to bear. Go it alone so he thinks all is well. And you? Binge to sooth the rising, fearful panic. Ages later, we finally had a heart-to heart and rediscovered that panic shared is panic dissipated.

A year later, almost to the day, I had that surgery for parotid cancer. This time, Ron broke his back in another work-related accident. Once again, that meant several weeks off work waiting for back surgery, recuperation, and full health. Never much of a complainer, I think even Ron struggled when lightning struck our home in the middle of this. It destroyed all our appliances. Then? Ron got diabetes. And me? I struggled to cope with my first flashbacks. With nothing to hold them down, those painful and traumatic memories exploded out of my subconscious and into my reality. Intensely vivid, they struck at any moment and returned at their own whim.

There is a story about a tired, worn-out mother who spent her days with her four preschool children, ages one and two, and a set of twins, age three. One day, Daddy brought home a six-week-old puppy for the children to love and Mommy to care for.

"Mommy, mommy, mommy, what shall we call our puppy?" the children cried.

She said, "You had better call that dog Mommy, because if it stays, I'm out of here!"

I thought someone had moved a puppy into my house. I thought I couldn't stand one more thing.

A few days later, I heard a speaker talk about his hard times. He and his wife had only fifteen dollars left to their name. She had an expensive ring that didn't quite fit her.

"God," she prayed, "I'm taking our last fifteen dollars and I'm getting this ring sized to fit me. It will be a covenant between You and me that things are going to get better."

She did just that and, yes, things did begin to get better.

"God," I cried, "I wish I had a ring as a covenant that things are going to get better."

Then I remembered reading in my morning devotionals that God doesn't meet everyone in the same way. I thought about Noah and his ark and Moses and his burning bush, and I quickly apologized.

"God, I'm sorry! I don't need a ring, but God, please, may I have a covenant with You that things are going to get better?"

I didn't tell anyone about my prayer. In fact, I chatted with friends after the church service while we made our way to lunch. Quite frankly, I simply forgot all about it.

Five days later, Hubby came home from work, got down on one knee, and asked, "Will you marry me?"

I thought he had lost it. We'd been married over thirty years. There is a romantic in our home and it's not me, okay?

He held out a twelve-karat gold wedding band that he'd found at his job at the local recycling plant. He placed it on my finger. It was a perfect fit.

And then, I remembered my prayer.

> Though the fig tree does not blossom and there is no fruit on the vine, though the produce of the olive fails and the fields yield no food, [though] the flock is cut off from the fold and there are no cattle in the stalls,

> yet I will rejoice in the Lord; I will exult in the [victorious] God of my salvation. (Habakkuk 3:17–18)

Could it be true? Was it really possible to thank God in the midst of pain, trouble, and suffering? Did God love me just as much in the hard times? I gently tread in the truth that the very same God who cared enough to die on the cross for my sin, cared enough to take care of me through the bad times as well as the good times.

I've had lots of opportunities to learn and relearn that lesson. Once, in the space of nine months, I moved into my parents' home to care for them, we had financial troubles, and my dear friend and sister-in-law, Jean, died.

Two other relatives died within days of each other. My husband lost his job twice, both times through company downsizing. Dad died and I had to sign Mom into a nursing home. One of our children almost died three times. I sorted and sold my parents' home, and then my mom died.

Honestly, some of those days I was living under the circumstances. Not because God was different, but just because I forgot that God is faithful in the good times, and that God is faithful in the bad times—and when the way is rough, your faith has a chance to grow.

My dear friend, Jean, collected fancy plates and loved pretty clothes. We often joked about being size tens together some day. (We were occasionally size tens, just never at the same time!) But on the day she died, I said to her, "None of it matters, does it, Jean? Not the clothes, not the dishes, not the size tens."

"No," she whispered. "None of it matters but Jesus."

Now, I don't know what is happening in your life, but I know this: Jesus is enough for whatever it is. Like my sister-in-law, we all come to our last day. What a shame it would be to find out that we've been chasing the wrong things. We can choose our path, but the path with Jesus on it is much easier to walk than the path we walk alone.

> The Lord God is my Strength, my personal bravery, and my invincible army; He makes my feet like hinds' feet and will make me to walk [not to stand still in terror, but to walk] and make [spiritual] progress upon my high places [of trouble, suffering, or responsibility]! (Habakkuk 3:19)

Jesus is enough. I don't need to be afraid anymore, because I learned that God is enough. I don't need to protect myself with fat and eating disorders anymore, because God is my protection. You, too, can have that freedom. Perhaps no one ever told you who Jesus really is.

Jesus is the Son of God. He died on the cross just for you, just for me, to pay the price for your sin and mine. He was raised from the dead, just for you, just for me. He's the mighty Son of God with the Holy nature of God Himself (see Romans 1:2–4).

CHAPTER SIX

"My unbelief must continually

amaze Jesus."

IN A CURIOUS WAY, TELLING set me free. Knowing that others knew about my habit gave me courage to walk a new path. From my telling moment on, I believed God could help me overcome my addiction. Me, a former slave, captive to bulimia for sixteen years, now walked in some freedom.

The journal never lies.

> This sounds wonderful on paper, but just as I'm getting used to yesterday, along comes today. Fear and depression continue. Past memories rain (or should I spell it reign?) over me, but I no longer have my purge escape mechanism. Addictive behaviours isolated my emotions. With that wall collapsed, my mind is in free fall.
>
> I've just learned that depression is anger turned inward. What a relief it is to realize

that I don't suffer from depression. I've misnamed my tangled emotions.

Depressed? No! I'm just plain angry! I think about confronting my abuser. I want to hurt him like he hurt me. I don't need antidepressants! I need a baseball bat, a revolver, and a sharp knife! Let me do damage to the one who damaged me! The only reason I won't land up in a jail cell is that he's already dead.

God started to point out that total freedom involves forgiveness. Verses like these kept showing up in my daily devotions:

Do not say, "I'll pay you back for this wrong!" Wait for the Lord, and he will deliver you. (Proverbs 20:22, NIV)

But if you do not forgive men their sins, your Father will not forgive your sins. (Matthew 6:15, NIV)

In anger his master turned him over to the jailers to be tortured, until he should pay back all he owed. This is how my heavenly Father will treat each of you unless you forgive your brother from your heart. (Matthew 18:34–35, NIV)

This one was the last straw:

And when you stand praying, if you hold anything against anyone, forgive him, so that your Father in heaven may forgive you your sins. (Mark 11:25, NIV)

Ever so slowly, God helped me to see that because He forgave my sin, my wrongdoing, He expected me to forgive the one who sinned against me. It seemed impossible, but God is the God of the impossible.

Eventually I reasoned that I had nothing to lose. My unforgiving attitude was only hurting and destroying me. I decided to take God at His word. I made a conscious effort to forgive. After all, how hard could it be? The guy was dead. I'd just love and forgive him from afar. I could do that.

Unfortunately, God had another plan. He pointed it out in Luke 6:27–33:

> But to you who are listening I say: Love your enemies, do good to those who hate you, bless those who curse you, pray for those who mistreat you. If someone slaps you on one cheek, turn to them the other also. If someone takes your coat, do not withhold your shirt from them. Give to everyone who asks you, and if anyone takes what belongs to you, do not demand it back. Do to others as you would have them do to you.
>
> If you love those who love you, what credit is that to you? Even sinners love those who love them. And if you do good to those who are good to you, what credit is that to you? Even sinners do that. (NIV)

God just would not let me escape those words. He suggested I go to the cemetery and lay hands and red roses on the abuser's tombstone. I told God exactly what I thought about his plan.

"I don't think so, God!" I screamed. "I have no intention of ever doing good deeds for that creature! Forget it."

Surprisingly, life went on and I continued to obey God in lots of other ways.

However, about twenty years later, circumstances placed me near that little cemetery town. Again, God spoke and terror filled my heart as I sensed his words: "Today would be a good day to go to the cemetery."

"Okay, God, I'll drive past the cemetery, but if the gate's locked I'm not going in."

Just to be sure, I prayed that the gate would be locked. Ha! Talk about unanswered prayer!

Then? "I don't know where the grave stone is, Lord. Sorry. Oh, and by the way, forget about me reading through a thousand tombstones!"

Sure that the grave would be impossible to find, I drove speedily through the grounds. God thought a slower meander would be more helpful. Sigh. I drove the gravel path again, this time slowly. There it stood right in front of me. Yuck.

Several minutes passed before I could force my trembling body out of the car and take my first hesitating steps. I fearfully placed my fingertips on the rim of the stone. A healing sensation, somewhat like an electric shock, ran through my body.

I tearfully prayed aloud. "Lord, I could have settled this with you so long ago. Forgive my disobedience. Thank you for healing me. You knew best all along. I forgive this man for what he did to me and likely to many others. God, I am so sorry I waited so long to obey. Oh, and God? God, I'm so sorry. I don't have any flowers."

I turned to walk back to my car and there, where my feet had trod but a few moments before, lay two silk roses.

"They will blow away, Lord," I whispered, "but I will put them over there anyway."

As I approached the stone for the second time, I noticed two small evenly spaced holes at its base. I slid the mauve flower into one—mauve for mourning, for surely God had mourned with me in the midst of the sins committed against me. I put the white one in the other hole—white for purity, because God had cleansed my heart of all its bitterness.

Relief flooded my being. Disobedience and unbelief had postponed my personal healing for a quarter of a century. I hadn't believed God enough to obey Him. Only my procrastination postponed the forgiveness that was really His gift to me.

CHAPTER SEVEN

"Technically, I was free from bulimia."

TECHNICALLY I WOULD NEVER perform the act of bulimia again. However, while the truth really did set me free, all kinds of emotions, bad habits, and thoughts needed conquering.

Matthew 13:22 points out that the worry of the world chokes us. I made a list of all my "worry hats." Most were duties I took on simply because I couldn't say no. For me, confrontation was a no-no. I hated confrontation and I avoided it at all costs, even when I ended up being the one who paid.

I begged God to help me live up to what others expected me to be. He refused.

His goal was a "be the best that she could be" Brenda. The trouble is, I didn't know what that gal looked like. I didn't know I wasn't me.

I tried to practice "eat and be satisfied," like the folks in Matthew 14:20: *"They all ate and were satisfied, and the disciples picked up twelve basketfuls of broken pieces that were left over"* (NIV).

I've never cared to binge on loaves and fishes. I doubt I ever will. Jesus didn't mention butter, or I could argue the point. But cake, chocolate, peanut butter? Eat and be satisfied? I no longer threw up guilt in the bathroom, but I continued to stuff down other emotions with food, in my kitchen, my car, and anywhere else I could get a little privacy.

> I read that bulimics who stop the act will gain about fifteen percent of their body weight; I anxiously await my fate, because if there is an average I am always above it. My weight issues and attitudes continue to be way out of balance. Dealing with life's stress without the bulimia is excruciating. I'd always blocked my feelings. Now, I want to get to a lower scale number, but they suffocate me. A storm of emotional tides run over me.

I refused to trust God when He began to point out what I should eat. The scale announced 177 pounds. I thought it was the end of the world. Years later, when I topped out at 224, I'd have braved a lava flow for that teeny number.

Friends and family flocked to my defense when the truth of my bulimia came out. They were on my side. A few admitted to the same behaviour. I could reach out for help now, but I didn't because I still didn't feel worthy of anyone's love or care, and that included God's. If He had offered me a miracle, I'd have asked Him how many were in line ahead of me.

Fear remained my guiding post. My irrational behaviors worsened. The unknown threw me into panic attacks. An invitation to coffee after a college class ended with me hiding in the bathroom, hyperventilating and talking myself into more "normal" behaviour.

I now did every task at least twice. Jury duty meant a practice run to the courthouse well ahead of time to find parking, the entrance, and the waiting rooms. A week later, I followed my practice plan to safety. A social invitation meant a trip to the event center to check out the location, the parking, and even the building.

And I continued to binge. The only difference was that I didn't purge anymore. Oh, what this did to my stomach, my weight, my emotions, and my sense of worth! My journals are full of pleading cries to God. Eventually, I topped out at 224 pounds. Or maybe it was more. I recorded that number after a week of lettuce.

> Help me! Help me, God. Help me out of this morass
> of emotions, attitudes, and actions. Why can't I stop
> this binging? Why do you help me in other things
> but not in this?

Bulimia still clutched me. No, I wasn't throwing up, but that's all that changed.

I kept my fears in check by binging on humongous quantities of food. Wound as tight as a child's spring toy, I worked hard for approval. This meant I could never say no. Quite simply, I was a bomb waiting to go off.

It didn't take much. A spilled glass of milk, an unmade bed, a slow driver ahead of me… all could provoke a scene. Sometimes it was exploding tears, occasionally a screaming mouth, but more often it was blistering silence—all of it un-expected and uncontrollable from my end.

I couldn't articulate my needs. As a child, I had skipped grades and recited at school concerts. The abuser and his actions changed all that. That wicked person stole not only my voice, but my very being. The other me learned safety in silence. It was my self-protection. Damaged goods don't expect kind treatment, and they don't get it.

Oh, I planned what I wanted to say. I'd get ready to tell that committee lady that I couldn't bake all the cookies for the sale again this year. It was no use. When that phone call came, my mouth opened and out would come those mealy-mouth words: "How many dozen do you want?"

I couldn't say no. No, not even to a total stranger who wanted a sitter. Here is the journal's version of a conversation with a mom I'd never met before.

"If you want to visit your family, why don't you just go?" I asked.

Oh, silly me with "stupid" plastered on my forehead. I presumed that she would do what I would do. Pack diapers, tuck the one-year-old under her arm, and get on the bus/train/plane.

"I have no one to look after the baby," she moaned.

I felt like the creator of a cartoon strip called "Watch Brenda Run Herself Over One More Time." My mouth moved and my ears heard these words.

"I'll take him."

What was that? Who said that? Why did she say that?

And Mom plunks her babe at our house on the very week our children go to my brother and sister-in-law's for a holiday. This is also the same week that babe discovers his screaming voice. Poor Ron comes home from a long day at work, expecting peace and quiet.

"Can't you make him stop that?" he groans, holding his ears.

"No, I can't," I sob. "He's been doing it all day."

I hit a new low one summer, when our home and back yard contained (all in the same week, at the same time) a couple of cousins settled into a tent trailer, in-laws enclosed in a travel trailer, my sister's two measled toddlers, my brother who didn't have a place to stay, and all the others who came to visit the first bunch! It's not like I didn't know it was happening. I had invited them.

I served dinner to at least nine people every day, and sometimes as many as twenty. I didn't ask for help. Why would I? Martyr Brenda shouldered everything herself.

> Bimbo (our collie) ran away from home and moved in to the neighbour's garage. I'm jealous. I want to go with him. My only physical escape is my job. I relish any opportunity to get out of the chaos at this house. I owe any emotional stability to the Dairy Queen. I eat ice cream on the way to work and I eat ice cream all the way home. It soothes the savage beast within me.

When Bimbo finally came home, I realized both of us had made it through. Another crisis averted, for the time being.

CHAPTER EIGHT

"The third day is a killer."

I'm coming off a three-day bender. A bender is a term alcoholics sometimes use to describe their drinking binges. "Bender" sure suits me. I'm bending the real me out of shape, terminating any current successes. This makes me fumble and I missed my finish line goal… a one-pound weight loss this week. Instead I let my mind recreate, and then re-enact, the hate I feel for my failing perfectionist self.

It's not like God doesn't know what I'm like. He's had lots of chances to see me in action. I am ashamed. A migraine pounds my brain while companion nausea massages my gut. The scale screams up because a week's worth of groceries disappeared into the abyss of my stomach. Today, I'm drying out and the feelings I savagely tamped down with both hands sprout forth into full blossom.

This is today's truthful scribblings. Forty years and I still occasionally succumb to emotional eating. Will I ever make better food decisions?

"The most important one," answered Jesus, "is this: 'Hear, O Israel: The Lord our God, the Lord is one. Love the Lord your God with all your heart and with all your soul and with all your mind and with all your strength." (Mark 12:29–30, NIV)

I'VE HEARD THAT SATAN, the evil one, works in the exact opposite way of God. If this is true, he first tries to sap my strength, then deluges my mind, corrupts my soul, and finally takes my heart captive. Really? I carefully analyze this last binge. Like thousands of others, it started long before the eating.

Strength is the physical power to carry out demanding tasks or deal with stressful or painful situations. A trusted friend lied. I should have confronted her, but I swallowed the pain. A relative's cutting comments and ignorant sayings continued. I held my tongue as my personal mind glue reached out and sucked everything to my being.

The next few days blurred. Long hours of writing deadlines, unexpected social events, babysitting, and doctor's appointments followed. I gave up my strength because I forgot to take care of my own health. Overtired and just plain weary, I became fair game for the hunter.

The dictionary defines the mind as the center of consciousness that generates thoughts, feelings, ideas, and perceptions and stores knowledge and memories. Instead of thinking good thoughts, enjoying pleasant feelings, or even getting a fresh idea or two, I'd allowed myself to wallow in painful past experiences.

The soul is the complex of human attributes that manifests as consciousness, thought, feeling, and will, regarded as distinct from the physical body. All my feelings operated in overdrive. I emotionally bled out. To compensate for that painful loss, I ate myself into oblivion. Did I like what I ate? No. Was the food tasty? I don't know. I didn't care. It passed the usual test. It was swallowable. I ate it so that I wouldn't feel anything.

Finally, the heart is the basis, the source, the center of one's emotional life. The deepest and sincerest feelings are located here, and here the person is most vulnerable to pain. I'd let myself get too busy to spend time with God. I'd ignored all of God's warning signs. My addiction wheeled out of control. I stumbled into failure because I neglected my health, dwelt on the past, tried to bury my emotions, and lived in pain, all the while neglecting my God. Yes, just like a drinking binge, these last three days were a killer. The sad thing is that I knew better.

Elijah confronted a wicked king, prepared an offering the Old Testament way, called down fire from heaven, killed 450 false prophets, prayed the end to a three-year-drought, and raced on foot against the king in his chariot, and won—all on the same day. You can read his story in 1 Kings 17–19.

Like Elijah, I was done for. I admit that my tortured few days paled beside his. No matter. We ended up in the same place. As it says in 1 Kings 19:4, *"I have had enough, Lord."*

> Anyone who's lost as much weight as I have over the years should be invisible by now. Is that my fear? Am I afraid that a smaller me will be invisible and therefore unseen and unheard in the world? Am I that desperate for others to empathize with my pain?

That's how we got the Twisted Sister. In the year of my Fifty Things to Do Before I Die (now better known to the world as the Bucket List), we drove to a "hot chocolate, sleigh rides, and carols" kind of tree farm, because I'd never been to one.

You traipse through snow to your elbows, spill hot chocolate on your good jacket, argue about which near-perfect tree is best, wear the kids out, and scratch the top of the car as you lash on a spruce tree two feet taller than your living room ceiling. Fun.

I spotted my tree as soon as we arrived. She stood alone in a bare patch of cut pines. It was easy to see why no one wanted her. She started out all right, but about halfway up the trunk it looked like an axe had bruised her and twisted her sideways. She resembled the L's a kindergarten child draws before they learn right angles. Oh, she tried to cover it up. A huge burl grew over the cut, but I saw it. I fell in love at first sight.

She looks just like me, I thought. *She started out like all the others, then some weird happening left its mark on her. She suffered and then made great efforts toward recovery but the mark still shows and nobody loves her because she isn't perfect. I will love her.*

It took but a few minutes to cut down our too-tall spruce and tie her onto the car roof. It took much longer to convince Ron that she was the one for us.

She didn't scratch us or the car at all, because she was so grateful to be picked. Ron wanted to shorten her up. I balked. Like me, I knew she needed to hang onto every part of herself so that she could make it through whatever came her way. She stood tall in the tree stand with her head bent ever so gently against the ceiling. We perched the treetop angel on a lower branch with the nativity scene below.

By the time we added lights, tinsel, and bows, she almost looked like all our other Christmas trees. Her sore spot was at eye level. Others could see it if they really looked, but somehow they missed it. They stared at what she had become. I concentrated on where she'd been.

I knew about her wounded past. I understood why wounds lingered. I expect they'll be there forever, no matter how she presents herself. Still, Twisted Sister fulfilled her destiny because somebody loved her. Twisted Sister gave me hope. Come January, I lamented her leaving. Part of me went with her. Now I was alone again.

I pondered that last three day binge by writing down everything I knew about three days.

> Three days of binging means your office party dress won't fit. In three days, every sign of spit and polish housework disappears. Leftovers seem to last forever or at least three days, whichever comes first, and we all know that both fish and company smell after three days.
>
> And Jesus rose from the dead on the third day after His crucifixion. What? Is it possible that three days can conquer both good and bad?

I always start a new diet on Monday. Success is guaranteed because I'm not at all hungry. Why would I be? I've been binging since Wednesday.

On Tuesday, I rise with enthusiasm because one slim day lies under my belt. By midday, I begin to slide but manage to hang on by having a little butter on my bread.

Wednesday brings a luncheon invitation. They serve salad, but I've had my fill of greens. I resolve to eat a teeny dinner to make up for my gargantuan lunch, but I succumb to the pizza Hubby brings home.

Thursday is Monday déjà vu. I have poached egg on toast for breakfast, even though I've already blown Wednesday.

Friday is another Tuesday, only this time it's a spoon or two of dessert.

On Saturday, the good hostess in me serves and eats the holiday meal.

Everyone knows that Sunday is a day of rest. Anyway, Monday is coming.

I picked up a magazine a friend had loaned me with the understanding that I would pass it along to someone else. I always rip the hard cardboard bits out of my own magazines and throw them away. As far as I'm concerned, they just irritate the reading experience.

I tried to keep her book intact. I really did, but those ads, order forms, and perfume samples drove me crazy. In no time, they were history. As my hand hovered over the garbage container, I sensed God whispering, "You have to do the hard bits."

"What do you mean 'the hard bits,' God?" I asked. "I start out every Monday morning with a gleam in my eye and a zip to my lip." I finished my own conversation before God could get a word in edgewise, then I ate until two o'clock in the afternoon.

Will I have a breakthrough if I make it through the third day without faltering? Is Day Three really the killer of all that hinders me?

What If?

You probably think I should be over this by now.
A lifetime of temptation, giving up, starting again—
Follow me into the turmoil of my mind.
My body will never be what I want it to be.
It's too late for my version of perfect.
Age eliminates firm arms, slender waist.

Truth broadcasts itself through my conscience.
What is left? Is it possible to set new goals?
Eliminate old thought patterns?
What if I aim not for perfect body, but loving heart?
What if I learn to care about me, like You do?
What if I see myself as You see me?
Precious, beloved, created for joy.
I am important in my speck of the world.
I am grateful for your patience with me
I begin again.

There will be a slight pause before Chapter Nine. I'm going to find out, one way or another.

CHAPTER NINE

"It is always the third day."

HURRAH! FOR ONCE, MY journal records success.

> I'm back. It is true. Day Three is a killer. I've not binged for four days. This is a record for me. Was it hard? Excruciatingly so. Was it worth it? Yes.
>
> I grasped the freedom that comes when I cling to Jesus with wild abandon. He rose from the dead on the third day, and so have I. Success, in spite of a spaghetti dinner at a friend's home, a birthday party, a buffet dinner, and a full day of shopping. I made hard choices, ate small amounts, and with Christ's help conquered the Mount Everest of my mind. I have a new sense of accomplishment, and awareness of past failures drops from my memory and soul.

Thousands of Christians are tortured daily for Christ. They don't refute Him, even in the face of certain death. I used to worry that if I was tortured, I'd cave at a whiff of chocolate. After all, I've done that nearly every day for a lifetime.

Today, I take courage from my morning Bible verse:

> Who satisfies your mouth [your necessity and desire
> at your personal age and situation] with good so that
> your youth, renewed, is like the eagle's [strong, over-
> coming, soaring]! (Psalm 103:5)

Thanks, God. You surely satisfied my mouth with good. On the third day, I finally tasted something better than Molten Lava Chocolate Cake. You.

Ron and I downsized our home when he retired. What if I downsized my body as an act of worship and sacrifice? What if the fear I wore as an emblem of failure became the courage of Christ in me as my God-given, precious body became what it was meant to be?

I'm tired of living like a wild animal, strolling where I shouldn't stroll, eating what I shouldn't eat, and being what I shouldn't be, all for the sake of having my own way.

Is it over? Am I free of the struggle? Following Jesus involves a lifetime of learning, commitment, and obedience in new places. Have I learned how? I pray I remember that every day is the third day. Every day is the day of the cross. The third day is power for resurrection or power to death.

> And whoever does not carry their cross and follow
> me cannot be my disciple. (Luke 14:27, NIV)

> For if we have been united with him in a death like
> his, we will certainly also be united with him in a
> resurrection like his. (Romans 6:5, NIV)

I cling to God's promise.

> For you were once darkness, but now you are light
> in the Lord. Live as children of light. (Ephesians 5:8,
> NIV)

After all, when God promises a thing, He means it.

When I read that Ephesians verse, I sensed that God meant I was already light in pounds, and that time and obedience could make this truth visible.

The word "light" can mean a source of brightness, coming to rest, weighing comparatively little, carrying a relatively low weight, moving with grace and agility, or making light of something.

The weight-minded me learned to make light of my life in public. Laughter protected me and helped me heal. I used it to steer conversations away from topics I couldn't face. I made fat jokes about myself before others could.

The dictionary says that laughter as an expression of mirth accompanied by certain convulsive, involuntary actions of the breathing muscles. Air is forced from the chest in a series of jerks, which produces short, abrupt sounds. Certain movements take place in the face and merriment is visible in the eyes.

How can something so much fun sound so dull? The Bible describes laughter this way:

> A cheerful heart is good medicine, but a crushed
> spirit dries up the bones. (Proverbs 17:22, NIV)

Or you could say that a joyful heart works a good healing, brings good improvement, and powerfully advances the recovery! I sure needed a little healing, some good improvement, and a powerful recovery in my life.

I decided to take up laughter on a regular basis when I discovered it actually increases blood flow and contracts the stomach muscles! Great! No more sucking in my gut, doing sit-ups, or wearing slippy control top, one-size-fits-all pantyhose. Every woman knows that one-size-fits-all means that one-size-fits-nobody!

One hundred belly laughs equal ten minutes on a rowing machine. It takes our mind off our troubles and our pain. Why, laughing even reduces the possibility of a heart attack. Watching a comedy boosts blood flow to the heart. It's equivalent to a bout of aerobic exercise or starting a cholesterol-lowering drug! Laughter is also a wonderful stress reliever. It is thought that one laugh burns six calories. Forget exercise. I'm concentrating my time on laughing!

I always wear a pedometer. Apparently, walking ten thousand steps a day gives you a longer life—at least, it seems longer to me. One day I wore it to a friend's house. It had eight thousand steps on it. I walked twenty steps into the house, sat down on a chair, and laughed for a couple of hours. When I walked out twenty steps, that thing had counted to 10,000. Doesn't that give new meaning to the phrase belly laugh?

CHAPTER TEN

"Let sleeping socks lie."

MY HUBBY AND I JUST celebrated our forty-eighth wedding anniversary. The last twenty or so years have been just swell!

You see, on the evening of our twenty-fifth wedding anniversary, I found myself once again on my hands and knees under the dining room table with my hands on Hubby's socks. Ron had a nasty habit of working his socks off his feet during dinner. You wouldn't know it. He made no suspicious looks or wriggling movements to show this was happening. Still, I always found myself on my hands and knees under the dining table, picking up those socks after dinner.

So here I was, on the floor, on my twenty-fifth wedding anniversary, with my hand on those socks. It suddenly came to me that if I continued to pick up those things, my future would continue to be the same as my present. I would be on my hands and knees every night, picking up socks. I caught a vision of myself at age eighty-four, trying to manoeuvre my walker close enough to use one of those little picker-upper-gadget things. I considered my dilemma for about two seconds, then made the decision to let sleeping socks lay.

That first night, I watched carefully as Hubby sat down. A look of surprise—you might even say shock—crossed his face. He said nothing. Hey, I said nothing! It took three nights and three pairs of socks. On the third night, he picked them all up and put them in the wash. It's another three-day victory story, because he's been doing that ever since.

While that one decision made a big difference in my life, it didn't have the same impact as another decision I made about thirty years ago. Someone told me how much God loved me. I didn't know He'd sent His only Son, Jesus Christ, to take the punishment for my wrongdoing. I didn't realize that His death on the cross provided life for me or that He had died so that I could live.

I didn't know He had risen from the dead, or that He lives right now. He defeated death.

It really was that simple. I broke the law. I was separated from God, but Jesus died and rose from the dead so that I could be forgiven. All I had to do was turn away from my sin and ask Jesus into my life.

However, I had to decide. Just like those socks under my table, I had to make up my own mind. Did I want a different life? Did I want to be free from my old life or not?

The Bible says our joy can be full.

> And we are now writing these things to you so that our joy [in seeing you included] may be full [and your joy may be complete]. (1 John 1:4)

And the joy of the Lord is our strength.

> Do not grieve, for the joy of the Lord is your strength.
> (Nehemiah 8:10, NIV)

It promises that there is great joy in heaven when a sinner repents.

> I tell you that in the same way there will be more rejoicing in heaven over one sinner who repents than over ninety-nine righteous persons who do not need to repent. (Luke 15:7, NIV)

And who would want to turn down the chance to make all of heaven rejoice?

When I asked forgiveness for my wrongdoing and asked Jesus into my life, God did forgive me. My life changed far more than it did with that pair of socks. God started to change me from the inside out. I couldn't live a good life all by myself. I just couldn't. My past, attitudes, addictions, temper, greed, desires, and myself got in the way

Recently, I heard about a wonderful travel tip. Pack your oldest but still presentable clothing. When you change, throw the used items into the hotel wastebasket. Your suitcase gets lighter every day. This makes sense. Why buy new clothes for people you will never see again?

I just happened to be preparing for my trip of a lifetime, a journey to Israel. All those old clothes with faded colour and weak elastic went into my bag. I did have some doubts. In fact, I got the "buts." But what would people think? But was it a Christian thing to do?

Then I read this Bible verse: *"Do not cast me off in the time of old age; forsake me not when my strength is spent"* (Psalms 71:9, RSV).

Fortunately, closer study revealed that the psalmist was not speaking about my old underwear. I admit the first outfit was a little painful, but I didn't know anyone in Israel. I moved to a different hotel every day. Only the chambermaid and I would ever know. If she snooped in the wastebasket, it served her right. And besides, she'd think they belonged to my roommate.

What a freeing experience! I dumped stuff I no longer needed, stuff that was just weighing me down. The Bible tells us to throw off everything that hinders and the sin that so easily entangles (see Hebrews 12:1). Surely that includes old clothes!

I shudder to think of where I'd be if it weren't for Jesus. He helped me get rid of the old me—my old clothes, if you will. The Bible says that God makes known the path of life and He fills us with joy when we are in His presence (see Psalms 16:11). Joy!

Since I made that life-changing decision to ask Jesus into my life, He's been teaching me how to be content and, yes, even joyful, in every situation. I learned that for every minute of binging, moping, whining, and complaining, I lost sixty seconds of happiness.

It is said that children laugh about four hundred times per day. Apparently, adults used to laugh nineteen minutes per day but now they average less than six minutes per day Sadly, some Christians laugh even less. Too many of us look like we've been teething on lemons since birth.

When I asked Jesus into my life, I slowly learned to be like a little child once more. Someone stole my childhood, but Jesus gave it back to me. I've learned to trust and to find contentment, joy, and laughter again.

The Bible says that those who go out with heavy hearts will come home laughing (see Psalm 126:5). Who wants to stay on the floor picking up socks when they can choose joy, laughter, forgiveness, and healing?

We all need someone to pay the price for our sin, our wrongdoing. That someone is Jesus. The good news is that He did it already, but just like me, you have to make that decision. Will it be old socks for the rest of your life? Or will you choose Jesus as your personal Saviour?

All you have to do is ask. Let's pray.

> Dear Lord Jesus,
>
> I confess that I am a sinner. Please forgive my wrongdoing.
>
> I believe that You are the Son of God and that You died on the cross to pay the price for my sin.
>
> I believe that You rose from the dead and that You are alive right now.
>
> Lord Jesus, please come into my life. Make me a member of your family.
>
> I now turn from going my own way. I want You to be the center of my life.
>
> Thank You for Your gift of eternal life.
>
> Thank You for Your Holy Spirit, who has come to live in me. Amen.

Did you pray that prayer with me? Then I welcome you into the family of God! Trust me. Your life will never be the same… and you will be glad!

CHAPTER ELEVEN

"We can decide which side of the ache

we will stand on."

YOU'VE HEARD MY STORY. The Bible says that even in laughter the heart may ache (Proverbs 14:13). That is true, but we can decide which side of the ache we will stand on. After years of experience, I know for sure that nothing, absolutely nothing, is too difficult to face when Jesus is our personal Saviour. He faces everything with us and even gives us joy for the journey. We can whine, complain, be angry, stay stuck in our addictions, or we can choose joy by choosing Jesus.

If you asked Jesus into your life, that is true for you, too.

> I've heard that the Nigerian name for God is "Father of Laughter." Why wouldn't He laugh? He conquered death and rose from the dead. He is coming again. Of course He is joyful. And He calls us to be joyful, too. Ron's cancer nurse insists that wellness is 90% attitude. We have the option to laugh… or cry.

Even illness and death have their funny side. One of my fondest memories is of my dad wearing one of those shrimpy blue hospital gowns, my black-and-white fake fur coat, and his winter boots. He held firmly to the nurse's desk with one hand and with the other he held a one-gallon container of fuzzy pink liquid that he had to down for a medical test. He stood with his legs desperately crossed, but his laughter joined ours. Unfortunately, this was too much for his tiny bladder, but just right for his sense of humour.

We often say things like, "We'll look back on this and laugh about it." Well, why not laugh about it today?

> A cheerful heart is a good medicine but a crushed spirit dries up the bones (Proverbs 17:22, NIV).

Maybe you're thinking that you have nothing to be joyful about. Mother Theresa said that we should never let anything make us so full of sorrow that we would forget the joy of Christ raised from the dead.

We can *"rejoice in the Lord always"* (Philippians 4:4, NIV). We can count it all joy when we meet troubles and we begin to get that joy when we ask Jesus into our life.

CHAPTER TWELVE

"Freedom is for those who take hold of it."

ONLY THE JOURNAL KNOWS.

> Some people find my scruples annoying. I inherited this really strong conscience from my mom, and Jesus topped it up. Clerk gives me too much change? I return it. Is another person's shopping cart in the middle of the field? I take it back into the store. Leave used paper towels on the bathroom floor? I'm your pick-up gal. I hip-hop my way around parking lots, stomping out flaming cigarettes butts before a bird ingests and dies or the same bird sets fire to your roof.

You might expect me to be the kind of person who doesn't get traffic tickets and you'd be right. Unfortunately, I got two the other day, on the same day, and within a few minutes of each other.

The first was for parking in a snow removal zone. I'm just a country gal, oblivious to city rules. Those signs meant nothing to me. My friend insisted on paying for that ticket. I left feeling pretty smug about the whole thing—because I'm not the sort of gal who gets tickets.

Ten minutes later, while driving past my grandchildren's school, I got a speeding ticket for $275 and three demerit points. As the officer handed me that second yellow slip of paper, I muttered, "You don't understand. I'm not the sort of person who gets tickets."

Then the officer and I glanced over to the passenger seat where that first ticket glared up at me.

Yellow tickets show up in my life when I forget who God is and who He says I am. I tried my best to be His best for twenty-five years. I served in all sorts of church positions and on church boards. I took every Bible Study available and then I taught them. I attended every conference within driving distance.

If I got one point for everything I did for Christ, I'd have ten divinity degrees on my wall.

> I read somewhere that handwriting with lower loops, no upward swing, and a hook to the left are signs of childhood abuse.
>
> What does this matter to me, really? I don't want it to matter, but it does. Right now I'm anxious, wondering the truth and yet not wanting to know it. Yes, I have residuals from abuse, bulimia being the smallest thing, but even my handwriting? That is annoying, upsetting, and devastating all at once.
>
> That the evil could permeate into every part of my body is almost too much to bear. The mere thought of it… I mean, how will I ever be free? Where will the "I" of me go?
>
> I never make spelling mistakes. Today my page is littered and I can't seem to make a capital "I" or even get an "I" into the word "will." Is that a clue?

My will demands that I (capital) take a turn at being strong and overtaking what is/has been/was for so long overtaking me.

The brutal truth descends. Yes, God helps me. Yes, the abuser is dead, but little "I" must grow up into big "I" and grab the truth. Freedom is for those who take hold of it.

Residual abuse issues continue to creep in to any good or happy part of my life. If others don't reject me, I reject myself. I play down every aspect of my faith. People can say what they like, but I know I must be a phoney. I don't seem to love like others love. I don't think I even love God. If I did, wouldn't I feel it? Know it? The Bible says that we love Him because He first loved us. Aha! He must not love me. That's why I don't seem able to love Him back.

One of my counselling sessions was particularly disturbing.

"What would you say if God told you that He had a gift for you?" asked the counsellor.

"I'd tell Him He made a mistake. It must be for the person in line in front of me."

The rest of the hour is a blank. I only remember her shocked face and my tears. Later, as I stumbled to the parking lot and started the car, God whispered one word into my heart that changed my life forever: "Beloved."

Beloved? Who? Me?

And I heard it again, this time with His interpretation.

B.e.l.o.v.e.d. Brenda,
You are B-eing
E-ternally
L-loved, and

O-verwhelmingly
V-alued.
You are E-ndlessly
D-ear to Me.

For the first time since becoming a Christian, I felt His accepting, welcoming love for me and I knew I loved Him in return. I always had. He'd always loved me, but I repelled His love because I thought it the only way to safety.

Recognising that I was His beloved made me feel really alive. Those yellow tickets had been in the way. Just like the folks in Mark 6:1–6, I hadn't taken God at His word. I needed to believe in His love, just like I believed in Him for my salvation.

That's My Girl

God, do You laugh when I scurry to and fro?
And waste my time in dithering?
Or giggle when I search the skies for glimpses of
      You?
Are You playing hide and seek with me
Just like I do with my children?

Are You easy to find?
Should I look harder?

No.

You cup Your ear to my cries,
Bend in my direction to better catch the sound,
Then You smile in recognition of my voice.
And brag into all ears…
"That's *my* girl!"

Our neighbour hadn't been able to help around the farm for years. When he died, his wife mourned, "If all he could do was sit in a chair, it was enough for me."

That's all I'd been expecting from Jesus. If all He could do was save me, it was enough for me. I settled for the least when He offered so much more.

CHAPTER THIRTEEN

"Now I live, truly live, in Christ."

So if you're serious about living this new resurrection life with Christ, act like it. Pursue the things over which Christ presides. Don't shuffle along, eyes to the ground, absorbed with the things right in front of you. Look up, and be alert to what is going on around Christ—that's where the action is. See things from his perspective. (Colossians 3:1–2, The Message)

A NEW PASTOR HAD TO conduct a funeral in a distant cemetery. He didn't know the area and got lost, arriving an hour late. The hearse and the family had already left, but the workmen were still there and the casket still uncovered. He decided to do the decent thing and conduct a service anyway. As he returned to his car, he heard one workman say to the other, "Do you think we should tell him it's a septic tank?"

Dead, just not buried; that's the Brenda I used to be. Now I live, truly live, in Christ.

We were in the middle of wedding preparations for our son and his bride-to-be when my husband got the doctor's diagnosis. Ron didn't make a sound until we got into the car. Then he took my hand and said these words: "We're not telling anyone till after the wedding. I won't spoil their day. I'm telling you, that's what I want."

I agreed to keep the secret, but I swallowed hard because I am the kind of gal who tells everyone everything.

I kept my mouth shut all right, but my eyes refused to stop leaking. Oh, but I cried. I cried everywhere Ron wasn't and some places where he was. At church, I wept into his shoulder during worship. I sniffled through sermons and sobbed through prayer. Those outside our secret knew only that our adult son was getting married. Since no one asked why I was wallowing in tears, I presume they all agreed that I must either hate my daughter-in-law to be, or love my son too much.

I wavered from joy to sorrow on a constant basis. Shower invitations cluttered the table while funeral thoughts filled my mind. I couldn't think straight. Tasks that previously flew through my fingers lay unfinished. Half-finished projects littered the house. Meals were scattered at best and downright inedible at worst.

I really let loose on my early morning walks. Practically galloping with stress, I'd pound my way around our little community screaming my anguish to God. I demanded He fix my life. I begged Him to restore Ron to health. I despaired at the thought of being without him. I wanted God to tell me how I'd manage.

"I've been married since I was eighteen, God. Our fortieth wedding anniversary is coming up. Tell me, God, are we going to make it?"

I paused on this. I stumbled on the curb. I just couldn't get a grip on the fact that our time together might soon be over. I'm ashamed to say that I kept up this routine for weeks. Finally, one morning I ran out of words. My voice and my tears dried up. My mind went quiet, too.

Into that deafening silence, God dropped these two words: "Choose life."

Choose life? What on earth did that mean? Would our circumstances change? Would Ron be healed? I vaguely remembered the phrase from a Bible passage and rushed home to look it up.

> This day I call the heavens and the earth as witnesses against you that I have set before you life and death, blessings and curses. Now choose life, so that you and your children may live. (Deuteronomy 30:19, NIV)

And I remembered once more to believe God.

> Be satisfied with your present [circumstances and with what you have]; for He [God] Himself has said, I will not in any way fail you nor give you up nor leave you without support. [I will] not, [I will] not, [I will] not in any degree leave you helpless nor forsake nor let [you] down (relax My hold on you)! [Assuredly not!] (Hebrews 13:5).

Our fiftieth wedding anniversary is now on the horizon. During the last ten years, Ron has had multiple bouts of chemotherapy, a hip replacement, and a triple bypass/valve repair. Yes, I have been known to panic a bit through some of this stuff, but never to the extent of that first life-threatening news.

make me to walk not stand still in terror

Brenda J. Wood

We live life in the present. We enjoy each moment with gratitude. We celebrate every doctor's report, whether good or bad. We recognize that everything passes through God's hands before it gets to us, and therefore it is life to us. We choose to see chemotherapy as our friend and I learned that a buttoned lip is not always a bad thing.

Will one of us die before the other? Likely. Yet that too has become life to us. We each have a personal relationship with Jesus and expect to meet again in heaven someday. So we go on, because God, who gives life, expects us to choose it.

> Though the fig tree does not blossom and there is no fruit on the vine, [though] the product of the olive fails and the fields yield no food, though the flock is cut off from the fold and there are no cattle in the stalls, yet I will rejoice in the Lord. I will exult in the [victorious] God of my salvation! (Habakkuk 3:17–18)

And this is followed by Habakkuk 3:19.

> The Lord God is my strength, my personal bravery, and my invincible army; He makes my feet like hinds' feet and will make me to walk [not to stand still in terror, but to walk] and make [spiritual] progress upon my high places [of trouble, suffering, or responsibility]!

I used to wonder how a high place could be one of trouble, suffering, and responsibility until I read Psalm 72:16.

> There shall be abundance of grain in the soil upon the top of the mountains [the least fruitful places in the land]."

The psalmist is right. In my hardest places, I've found God to be nearer and dearer than ever.

CHAPTER FOURTEEN

"How B.I.G. is your faith?"

A HUNGRY LION CHASED Brenda J. Wood along life's path. She struggled under her burdens of abuse and bulimia. The lion snapped at her heels. There was no way of escape. She was a goner.

> Be alert and of sober mind. Your enemy the devil prowls around like a roaring lion looking for someone to devour. (1 Peter 5:8 NIV).

Someone threw Brenda a rope—a Vine, if you will. She grabbed on to it with both hands and eventually trusted her body, with its burdens, to the Vine and safety. Only that Vine kept her from the lion's jaws.

> I am the vine; you are the branches. If you remain in me and I in you, you will bear much fruit; apart from me you can do nothing. John 15:5, NIV)

Brenda hung suspended in midair, clinging only to that vine. It was easier now that her burdens were on the

Vine and not on her back. Unfortunately, she slipped to the ground and into the near teeth of that lion many times, simply because she tried carrying everything herself. Eventually she learned that the Vine offered the only permanent safety. She got so attached to the Vine that she became one of its branches.

Finally Brenda noticed <u>fruit called Love and Joy on that Vine</u>. She picked some, ate it, and recognised that it had been there all along. All she had to do was <u>reach out and take</u> it. Because <u>the Vine called her Beloved</u>, she began to <u>yield fruit, too, fruit that came from the Vine</u>, onto her branch. Still, occasionally the Vine had to remind her that He was seeking righteous fruit, not a religious nut.

My poem has a new ending.

The Dieter's Lament

The sleeves are bulging in my dress.
My bra is double-rolled.
The calories I ate at lunch
Have multiplied untold.
My pantyhose are at half-mast
And cutting off my veins.
My extra fifty pounds or so
Are giving knee joint pains.

My waistline is herniated
By the elastic in my dress
And as I speak, a button pops,
My own fault I do confess.
My underwear is crying out
From definite overstrain.
My arches falling to my sole
Surely need a crane

When waving bye to all my friends,
My arm did slap my face.
I've switched to slip-on shoes this week.
I can't reach to tie a lace.
What is the cause of this mutilation
Of body, heart, and soul?
It is greed and self-destruction.
It's licking every bowl.

It is heartless condemnation
Of the real me, my goal.
It's eating, never thinking,
As I pile roll on roll.
If life is but three score and ten,
And I am halfway through it,
If thin is what I cherish,
Then I want to get me to it.

So this is me, my pain, my bod.
Now is the time to start.
I throw aside bulimia.
From gluttony depart.
I'll track what goes into my mouth
and watch for sneaky bits.
Give up extra portions
and butterscotch delights.

I put my tongue against my teeth
and say n-n-n quite clearly.
I form an "O" with both my lips.
There! I have it, nearly.
No-no-no! That basic word
that puts me on the path
To body slight and self-delight
And no more poundly path.

But as my body slims away,
On this you can be sure,
That as I get me to it,
With Christ I will endure.
Size twelve may own my closet
and twenties disappear,
And I will face life gladly,
Even in the mirror.

Someone told me that Christians should think, believe, pray, and act big. It took me ages to figure out that big simply means "Believe in God." I've finally learned to do that and I pray you will too.

I waited patiently and expectantly for the Lord; and He inclined to me and heard my cry. He drew me up out of a horrible pit [a pit of tumult and of destruction], out of the miry clay (froth and slime), and set my feet upon a rock, steadying my steps and establishing my goings.

And He has put a new song in my mouth, a song of praise to our God. Many shall see and fear (revere and worship) and put their trust and confident reliance in the Lord. (Psalm 40:1–3)

BULIMIA: WHAT IT IS

The term bulimia[4] describes insatiable, secretive eating binges followed by self-induced vomiting, laxative abuse, and/or fasting to rid the body of the food. It's shocking to hear people joke about "catching" bulimia till they lose a few pounds. If only they realized how remarks like this cheapened my pain. Believe me, if bulimia was "catching," I wanted to be released from its trap.

My parents were the average, normal kind. I was a good scholar, but at the same time I was introverted and achievement-oriented. I feared what people might think, so I kept the secret locked away. Even though I hated everything about the disease, I also feared living without the one coping mechanism I knew.

If you or anyone you know appears to have an eating disorder, go to a doctor, dietician, nutritionist, or therapist immediately. If you have been abused and no one believes you, keep telling your story until you find someone who does believe you and will take you seriously.

---

4   Note that these lists only include my personal experiences.

For you were once darkness, but now you are light in the Lord. Live as children of light (for the fruit of the light consists in all goodness, righteousness and truth) and find out what pleases the Lord. Have nothing to do with the fruitless deeds of darkness, but rather expose them. It is shameful even to mention what the disobedient do in secret. <u>But everything exposed by the light becomes visible—and everything that is illuminated becomes a light. (Ephesians 5:8–13, NIV)</u>

I concentrated on my weight, food, and calories too much. I used unhealthy behaviours to control my weight.

You need to know that:

- Eating disorders aren't new and have been around for centuries.
- Eating disorders involve physical, mental, emotional, and social conditions.
- Eating disorders take several different forms.
- Eating disorders generally require professional treatment.

My physical side effects included:

- Tooth decay, loss of tooth enamel, and other dental problems.
- Chronic indigestion, constipation or dehydration, and urinary tract infections.
- A hiatus hernia.
- Frequent weight fluctuations of ten to fifteen pounds.
- Irregular menstrual periods, and a hysterectomy.
- Swollen glands, a chronic sore throat, repeated throat infections.

- Facial puffiness, bloodshot eyes, bags under the eyes, and broken blood vessels in the eyes and face.
- Fatigue; disturbed sleep; dry, tender skin; and a rapid or irregular heartbeat.
- Disappearing after a meal, withdrawing from activities, and isolating myself from friends.
- Depression and irritability.

My emotional distress included:

- Guilt or shame because of lies, secrecy, and the financial waste of the binges.
- Obsession with food and personal weight.
- Overeating when under stress.
- Feeling out of control and unable to stop.
- Personality disorders like OCD (obsessive-compulsive disorder).
- Body dysmorphic disorder (too much focus on some body part or body shape seen as defective).

Consequently, I:

- Avoided eating when hungry.
- Felt guilty after eating.
- Was preoccupied with getting thinner.
- Went on eating binges and couldn't stop.
- Was overly concerned about calories, fat content of foods, and food in general.
- Was a perfectionist, overachiever, felt not good enough and worthless.
- Generally chose diet foods.
- Avoided foods with sugar, high fat, or carbohydrate content.
- Saw food as "good" or "bad."

- Sought approval from others, and had a difficult time saying no.
- Was preoccupied with body fat.
- Was seen as the "strong" one, expected to solve everyone's problems.
- Vomited after eating.
- Thought constantly about food, exercise, and calories.
- Expected life to be better, for others to like me more if only I lost weight.
- Took pride in being able to deprive myself of food.

Signs that I was susceptible to bulimia:

- Had weight concerns or behaviour problems before age fourteen. (I was six when I first started to worry about my weight.)
- Had high levels of perceived stress, and distressing life events during last year.
- Had a history of dieting.
- Had a negative personal evaluation, was shy and anxious.
- Was a perfectionist.
- Experienced parental control, sibling rivalry between siblings over shape or appearance.
- Heard critical comments about weight, shape, and eating from family members.
- Was teased about weight, shape, or appearance.

My Personal Experience

Bulimia is a vicious cycle of binging, purging, and vomiting. It consumed me for almost sixteen years, the last four after I asked Jesus into my life. I promised myself after every bout that I'd never buy or use laxatives or vomit again, only to repeat the cycle several times a day.

I was two different people. One? Fully in control, with marriage, career, and children all perfect. The other? A weak-willed, gobbling, out of control loner, stuffing down feelings of anger in the kitchen and throwing up guilt in the bathroom.

I asked people to pray about my weight loss, but I never confessed to the abuse or the bulimia. I feared what others would think.

Bulimics tend to have low self-esteem and a need to control and be perfect in every way. I often wonder how today's "supermom" image affects the closet bulimic. None of us will ever measure up to the standards set by today's society. Superwomen only live in comic books.

When I finally admitted to the bulimia, on a TV show with thousands of viewers, I began to get well. Truth is always the beginning of healing.

My finest resources are still my Bible and my journal. Everything is less threatening on paper. I've lowered my perfectionist standards a notch or two. I allow myself to be an average woman, better at some things than others. The two of me have become one, by the grace of God.

I suffer some after-effects. I sleep with the head of the bed elevated to prevent acid flow up my esophagus. I had a hysterectomy, which apparently is a common occurrence among bulimics. However, my frequent bouts with laryngitis disappeared.

If you are bulimic, make the decision to stop now. Please get medical attention. Make a concentrated effort to spend time with God. Leave yourself open to Him. Allow Him to take away the pain, guilt, anger, and low self-esteem. See yourself through His eyes. You are the Child of a King and He is the Great Healer.

> He heals the broken-hearted and binds up their wounds. (Psalm 147:3, NIV)

> But he was pierced for our transgressions, he was crushed for our iniquities; the punishment that brought us peace was on him, and by his wounds we are healed, (Isaiah 53:5, NIV)

Treatments may include behaviour modification, drug therapy, and in-depth counselling.

I don't know much about other treatments, but I do know what helped me. I've included a list for your information.

1. There is absolutely no substitute for knowing Jesus as personal Saviour. *"While Jesus was in one of the towns, a man came along who was covered with leprosy. When he saw Jesus, he fell with his face to the ground and begged him, "Lord, if you are willing, you can make me clean"* (Luke 5:12, NIV). We may not have leprosy, but we have our own kind of untouchable disease.

2. Pray for guidance. God does not meet everyone's needs in the same way. Seek His plan for you. *"For I know the thoughts and plans that I have for you, says the Lord, thoughts and plans for welfare and peace and not for evil, to give you hope in your final outcome"* (Jeremiah 29:11).

3. Pray specifically! About to make my first television appearance, I feverishly prayed that God would "make me thin on TV." My weight dropped not one iota. However, at the host's

request, I appeared regularly, documented my weight loss, and literally "got thin" on TV.

4. Expose both abuse and eating disorder to the light. Tell a friend, a doctor, a teacher—someone—about your situation. Keep telling until somebody believes you. As soon as I went public, I was free of the habit. I was tempted for a while, yes, but I never followed through on the actual deed. Remember God's promise in 1 Corinthians 10:13—*"No temptation has overtaken you except what is common to mankind. And God is faithful; he will not let you be tempted beyond what you can bear. But when you are tempted, he will also provide a way out so that you can endure it"* (NIV).

5. Face your feelings honestly. I thought I was only angry at the abuser, but in reality my anger was also directed at the people who should have protected me. I was also angry at myself.

6. Stop dieting. Rigid rules about "good" and "bad" foods make the problem worse. Remember, weight is not the problem. By the way, bulimia is not an effective weight-loss program. The amount of food purged never compensates for what stays in the body.

7. Make healthier food choices. Eat regularly throughout the day. Lower your fat intake. Drink six to eight glasses of water daily. We often think we're hungry when we're really thirsty.

8. Stay off the scale. The problem is not your weight. Deal with the problem, not the symptoms.

9. Exercise regularly. Exercise doesn't have to mean spandex, gyms, and step boxes. A thirty-minute walk is fine. Exercise increases the body's production of endorphins, which are natural pain and stress reducers.

10. Get in touch with your emotions. Allow yourself to feel anger, disappointments, and fear. Stop stuffing them down with food. Like a beach ball, they will always bob back up.

11. Read everything you can find on the subject. Ask God to open doors for you. Your church or library may be able to recommend books and other helpful resources.

12. Focus on the present. Stop dwelling on the past. Think the thoughts that Paul recommends in Philippians 4:8—*"Finally, brothers and sisters, whatever is true, whatever is noble, whatever is right, whatever is pure, whatever is lovely, whatever is admirable—if anything is excellent or praiseworthy—think about such things"* (NIV).

13. Do more of what works and less of what doesn't. Feel a binge coming on? Pray, go for a walk, or call a friend.

14. Give up on perfection. We aren't perfect; we never were and we never will be. Perfectionism makes us hard to live with and it's an impossible standard anyway. Only Jesus was perfect.

15. Don't let temporary failure or relapses get you down. Consider Habakkuk 3:17–18—*"Though the fig tree does not bud and there are no grapes on the vines, though the olive crop fails and the fields*

produce no food, though there are no sheep in the pen and no cattle in the stalls, yet I will rejoice in the Lord, I will be joyful in God my Savior" (NIV). We can choose how we will respond to our life situations. Praise the Lord, whatever your circumstances are, and remember that His love for you is unconditional.

16. Keep a journal. Record your feelings, whatever the Lord is doing in your life, and any steps, however small, you take toward healing.

17. Be obedient to what the Lord shows you. Truth is never really ours until we act on it. We humans find it easier to hang out on the same old path, but real change takes hard work.

18. Remember that God is faithful. He never does anything halfway. Patiently let Him set the timeframe as He leads you through the steps to wholeness. And there is wholeness.

As for you, you were dead in your transgressions and sins, in which you used to live when you followed the ways of this world and of the ruler of the kingdom of the air, the spirit who is now at work in those who are disobedient. All of us also lived among them at one time, gratifying the cravings of our flesh and following its desires and thoughts. Like the rest, we were by nature deserving of wrath. But because of his great love for us, God, who is rich in mercy, made us alive with Christ even when we were dead in transgressions—it is by grace you have been saved. And God raised us up with Christ and seated us with him in the heavenly realms in Christ Jesus, in order that in the coming ages he might show the incomparable riches of his grace, expressed in his kindness to us in Christ Jesus. For it is by grace you have been saved, through faith—and this is not from yourselves, it is the gift of God—not by works, so that no one can boast. For we are God's handiwork, created in Christ Jesus to do good works, which God prepared in advance for us to do. (Ephesians 2:1–10, NIV)

SUGGESTED READING

This is a small and quite incomplete reading list of books that helped me. Of course, the first book on any reading list is always the Bible.

 Cameron, Julia. *The Writing Diet* (New York, NY: Penguin, 2007).

Foster, Richard. *Celebration of Discipline* (New York, NY: Harper & Row, 1978).

Leaf, Dr. Carolyn. *Who Switched Off My Brain?* (Rivona, South Africa: Switch On Your Brain, 2007).

Leman, Kevin. *The Firstborn Advantage* (Grand Rapids, MI: Revell, 2008).

MacDonald, Gordon. *Ordering Your Private World* (Nashville, TN: Oliver-Nelson, 1985).

Meyer, Joyce. *Beauty for Ashes* (New York, NY: Time Warner, 2003).

Meyer, Joyce. *Battlefield of the Mind* (New York, NY: Time Warner, 2004).

Meyer, Joyce. *The Secret Power of Speaking God's Word* (New York, NY: Warner Faith, 2004).

Moore, Beth. *Get Out of that Pit* (Nashville, TN: Integrity, 2007).

√ Moore, Beth. *Breaking Free* (Nashville, TN: LifeWay, 2006).

√ Moore, Beth. *Believing God* (Nashville, TN: Broadman & Holman, 2004).

Wood, Brenda J. *Heartfelt, 366 Devotions for Common Sense Living* (Blind River, ON: Alloway's Printing & Publishing, 2009).

✱ Wood, Brenda J. *God, Gluttony and You* (Blind River, ON: Alloway's Printing & Publishing, 2009).